CAREERS
FOR
FINANCIAL MAVENS
& Other
Money Movers

VGM Careers for You Series

CAREERS FOR

FINANCIAL MAVENS
& Other
Money Movers

Marjorie Eberts
Margaret Gisler
with Mary McGowan
and Maria Olson

VGM Career Horizons
NTC/Contemporary Publishing Group

Library of Congress Cataloging-in-Publication Data

Eberts, Marjorie.
    Careers for financial mavens & other money movers / Marjorie
Eberts and Margaret Gisler with Mary McGowan and Maria Olson.
        p.   cm. — (VGM careers for you series)
    ISBN 0-8442-6316-8 (cloth). — ISBN 0-8442-6314-1 (pbk.)
    1. Finance—Vocational guidance—United States. 2. Financial
services industry—Vocational guidance—United States.   I. Gisler,
Margaret. II. Title.   III. Series.
HG181.E285   1998
332.6′023′73—dc21   98–26318
                                                          CIP

We would like to dedicate
this book to the financial
gurus in our families—Les,
Marvin, Ken, and Shari.

Published by VGM Career Horizons
A division of NTC/Contemporary Publishing Group, Inc.
4255 West Touhy Avenue, Lincolnwood (Chicago), Illinois 60646-1975 U.S.A.
Copyright © 1999 by NTC/Contemporary Publishing Group, Inc.
Printed in the United States of America
International Standard Book Number: 0-8442-6316-8 (cloth)
                                     0-8442-6314-1 (paper)
18   17   16   15   14   13   12   11   10   9   8   7   6   5   4   3   2   1

Contents

Acknowledgments

We wish to thank Mary McGowan and Maria Olson for substantial help in the writing of this book. Mary wrote Chapters 3, 9, and 10 and contributed interviews to Chapter 11. Maria is responsible for the copy in Chapter 2.

CHAPTER ONE

Careers for Financial Mavens

M oney is just pieces of paper labeled one dollar, ten pesos, or one hundred yen, yet it enables people to obtain food, clothing, cars, computers, and all the other goods of life. We accept money for our labor in fast food restaurants, steel mills, and department stores. We save it in banks and invest it in stocks, bonds, and other securities. The United States government spends trillions of dollars running the country, and General Motors and Coca-Cola earn billions from selling their products. There are not too many activities in the modern world that are totally divorced from money. Colleges accept it for tuition, and theaters accept it for admission. You may have used it to purchase this book. "Money makes the world go round" is far more than a line from a popular song.

Everyone, except for the hermit on a desert island, is involved in some way with money, but some people are absolutely fascinated by it. They turn to the financial pages before the sports section to see if they made or lost money in the stock market. They would rather watch television programs about inflation, the Federal Reserve, and government deficits than a popular sitcom. They know the monetary views of economists like Adam Smith and Alan Greenspan. They study ways to save money and try to find the best buys for their money. These people are financial mavens who are truly knowledgeable about money.

As children, financial mavens and other money movers counted pennies and actually saved money in their piggy banks. They were little entrepreneurs making money at lemonade stands in front of their homes. At an early age, they learned how to make budgets and delighted in allocating their funds. These young money movers opened savings accounts in banks as soon as they started earning money. As they became older they followed the ups and downs of stock from McDonald's to Microsoft. And they probably learned to do spreadsheets on the computer before they could word process. Today, many of these fledgling financial wizards are beginning to explore what they will do with their lives. Money and the world of finance continue to fascinate them, and they would like to pursue a career that involves working with money in some way. Fortunately, there are a great number of careers that will let them handle, count, invest, collect, and even make money.

A Quick Look at Jobs for Money Movers

When money movers begin to look for careers that offer them the opportunity to spend their days working in some way with money, an amazing number of possibilities will emerge. They'll find jobs are available in accounting firms, brokerage firms, banks, businesses, and the government. They'll discover that they could be bookkeepers, cashiers, tellers, accountants, and even Wall Street wonders managing portfolios worth millions of dollars before they are thirty. They could even combine their fascination with money with another career choice by becoming a tax lawyer or a detective solving cases of financial fraud.

This book is designed to help financial mavens and other money movers discover careers that will allow them to spend their days working with money in some way. Here is a glimpse of some of the careers that you will read about in this book.

Keeping Track of Money

Accounting professionals keep track of what people, businesses, the government, and organizations are doing with their money. They are both money and number people who do far more than record income and outgo on spreadsheets. They may concentrate on tax matters, create budgets, prepare financial reports, analyze financial information, check for waste and fraud, and consult on financial matters. As an accounting professional, you can choose to have your own business; work for a public accounting firm, from ones that have just a few employees to those who employ thousands; or be employed by businesses, organizations, or the government. You can work anywhere in the world as an accounting professional, but you will find the most jobs in large cities. To enter this profession, you will need a bachelor's degree in accounting or a related field. To gain professional recognition, you will find it helpful to become a Certified Public Accountant (CPA).

Helping People Buy and Sell Stocks

Every day investors buy millions of dollars of stock. Most people aren't experts so they rely on the help of securities sales representatives, more commonly known as a stockbrokers, to help them find the best investments. In this job, you won't actually buy or sell stocks and other securities for your clients, but you will place their orders with your firm's traders. A great part of your time will be spent researching the market and helping your clients devise portfolios that meet their needs, from money for retirement to funds for their children's education. Securities sales representatives usually work at brokerage houses from large nationally known firms like Merrill Lynch to smaller local and regional firms. In order to enter this profession, you have to meet state licensing requirements, which involve passing tests, to become registered representatives. Here is a career that lets you spend your days watching the gyrations of the stock market as you study how money is being invested throughout the world.

Buying and Selling Stocks

Traders are the individuals who are involved in the actual buying and selling of stock. Many spend their days on the floor of stock exchanges that are crowded, noisy, paper-littered workplaces. The brokers and traders are yelling out prices and jockeying for position. Things move so fast that million dollar transactions are completed in just seconds. Traders also work at brokerage houses, banks, mutual fund companies, investment banks, and other financial institutions. No matter where they work, the action is always frenzied. This is one job in which you will never stop working from the time the opening bell of the New York Stock Exchange rings until it rings again to signal the market is closed.

Managing Large Amounts of Money

Some organizations have enormous amounts of money that need to be invested. You could get a job at a college, a union, a foundation, or a corporation managing this money. Or you could get a job at a mutual fund that invests other people's and organizations' money. The financial mavens who have the responsibility for investing millions of dollars are known as portfolio managers. It is their job to increase the worth of portfolios through the shrewd sale and purchase of stocks, bonds, and other securities. A portfolio manager may manage one or more investment portfolios. These money movers devise an investment strategy for each portfolio they manage, which requires spending considerable time on the job gathering information. They have to know what is happening at companies in which they have invested and plan to invest and what is going on in the stock market.

Helping People Manage Their Money

When people begin to figure out what to do with their money, so many questions arise: How much insurance do I need? What can we afford to pay for a home? How should we budget the family income? What can I do to save more money? How can I get out of debt? What type of investments will best meet the needs of our family? Financial planners are the money experts who help people make solid decision in managing their money. Some are generalists who give across-the-board advice, while others are specialists who give advice in areas such as taxes, debt counseling, or retirement. If you elect to become a financial planner, you will usually establish your own business or work for a financial advisory firm. As states do not regulate financial planners, you will want to become a Certified Financial Planner (CFP) in order to indicate your competence in this career area.

Working at a Bank

The business of banking is money, which makes careers in this area an excellent choice for financial mavens. At banks, money movers who work as tellers have the opportunity to actually handle money. Besides traditional services, such as cashing checks and taking deposits, the job of teller has expanded to selling customers on new bank products and services from ATM cards to online banking. Tellers can advance to management positions in banking; however, most of these positions are filled by college graduates who have entered this career as management trainees. While bankers used to work just in banks, you'll now find them in mini branches in grocery stores and on malls. Many also work in savings and loan associations and credit unions that perform many of the same services as banks.

Raising Money for Businesses

Venture capitalists and investment bankers raise money for businesses. Venture capitalists help them get started, while investment bankers help established businesses get the money they need to expand their operations in some way. These are two professions that require you to have the highest qualifications in order to get a job. You will need to be a college graduate with an impressive work record and/or extracurricular activities. Venture capitalists and investment bankers usually start as analysts and spend considerable time in training as they learn to do their jobs. Both careers are fast paced and require people who can work well under pressure.

Working in Business Finance

Every business, no matter how small, has someone handling the money. Businesses must know how much money they are spending and earning. While in a small firm the owner will usually do all the financial work, as businesses grow individuals are hired to do more and more of this work. In large firms, there will be many departments with hundreds of workers handling the financial side of the business. Many of these departments will be concerned with accounting activities and headed by an accountant. The senior financial managers in businesses are the chief financial officers (CFOs), treasurers, and controllers. The controller is in charge of all the accounting departments and directs the preparation of all financial reports. Treasurers are responsible for the receipt, disbursement, and safekeeping of corporate moneys.

Handling Money for the Government

One in six people in this country works for the government. With the government spending trillions of dollars each year, many of these employees are money movers who manage, budget, and distribute money as well as collect it in federal, state, and local government jobs. From economist to clerk, government is a perfect place for financial mavens to find jobs. You can sell stamps in post offices, pay the military, make sure banks are being run properly, check the accuracy of tax returns, and supervise the collection of revenues. Money movers in the government are also busy minting money, looking for counterfeit money, printing paper money, and even destroying unfit money. In any government job, you will receive excellent benefits.

Finding Even More Jobs

With money playing such an important role in our economy, the number of jobs that involve money forms a very, very long list. In the last chapter of this book, we provide financial mavens and other money movers with information about even more careers. You'll learn about such jobs as cashier, tax lawyer, property manager, and financial writer. The more you notice where money is being handled and financial services offered, the more job opportunities you will be able to observe. Just think of the path that the dollar bill you spend for a soft drink takes before it is finally destroyed as an unfit bill. From the grocery store, it may go to someone who uses it along with other money to buy a bicycle and then to someone who deposits it in a bank until someone writes a check and receives it back as cash and may even buy a soft drink.

Job Qualifications

Financial mavens and other money movers want to find jobs in which they can be involved in some way with money. A few of these jobs require only a high school diploma, but most will require training or further education. The better you can handle numbers, computers, and business concepts, the better you will be prepared for jobs in the financial arena. Expect also to get licenses or certification to demonstrate your expertise to handle some of these jobs. Those of you who land the best jobs will often have had some previous work experience.

Searching for Your Dream Job

There are literally hundreds of ways to go about searching for your financial dream job. If you are still in school or a graduate of a school, the career center at the school will have listings of job openings. It is also a good place to start a job search, as you will be able to get sound advice on looking for jobs, handling interviews, and writing resumes. One way to meet a lot of employers at once is by attending a job fair. Be sure to take multiple copies of your resume, be dressed to impress, and be prepared to have a screening interview.

In this age of computers, more and more people are finding jobs by going on-line. Visit the Web sites of companies that interest you and study their listings of job openings. Look at your state's employment Web site, and be sure to visit on-line sites like the following that list thousands of jobs:

http://www.monsterboard.com/

http://www.4work.com/

http://yahoo.com/business/employment/

Don't forget traditional job searching techniques, which include reading want ads in newspapers and professional journals and using an employment agency. Finally, make sure that you network. Many financial mavens and other money movers have found jobs because they talked to family, friends, and coworkers.

CHAPTER TWO

Keeping Track of Money
The Job of Accountants and Auditors

T he practice of accounting has existed for thousands of years. Account books of various forms can be traced back to as early as 3500 B.C. At that time, scribes in ancient Babylon and Sumer were charged with the responsibility of recording commercial transactions, which they engraved in clay tablets. Because these initial accountants were among the few who could read and write in society, much of our current knowledge of daily life in ancient times has been drawn from accounting records. While present-day accountants are still responsible for the recording of financial events, their tools have changed. They are now using both mainframe and personal computers to keep track of financial information.

The Accounting Profession

Accounting professionals keep track of what the world is doing with money. Millions of businesses, governmental units, and individuals rely on their work. Accountants and auditors prepare, analyze, and verify financial reports and taxes and monitor information systems that furnish financial information to managers in business, industry, and government organizations. They are both investigators and reporters who work within the four major fields of accounting: public accounting, management accounting, government accounting, and internal auditing.

All accountants are certainly not alike, but they do share certain characteristics. As a financial maven interested in accounting, take the following quiz to see if you possess the qualities needed in this profession.

- Are you a numbers person with solid math skills?

- Are you able to pay close attention to details?

- Can you handle responsibility with limited supervision?

- Are you disciplined?

- Are you logical?

- Do you have good organizational skills?

- Are you able to interpret facts and figures quickly?

- Can you communicate complex material effectively both orally and in writing?

- Are you able to concentrate for long periods of time?

- Are you willing to work long, hard hours to get a job done?

- Are you a computer guru who is a spreadsheet expert?

- Are you willing to acquire the advanced education and certification required for this profession?

- Do you have high standards of integrity?

If you answered "yes" to many of these questions, then read on.

The Work Environment

Accounting professionals work for the corner deli operator as well as for fast-food giants, for the smallest municipal government and the federal government, and for you and me and Bill Gates. They work throughout the country, with the heaviest concentration of job opportunities in large urban areas, where many public accounting firms and the headquarters of many organizations and businesses are located. More than 20 percent of all accountants are employed in Chicago, Los Angeles, New York City, and Washington, D.C.

Individuals in this profession usually have desk jobs and generally work a forty-hour week. However, they frequently work much longer hours when reports or tax returns are due. Seventy-hour weeks are not uncommon. Those who are employed by public accounting firms and government agencies may travel frequently to perform audits at clients' places of business. Self-employed accountants, as well as those who work for small firms, may be able to do part of their work at home.

Getting Started in an Accounting Career

Beth Painter currently works for a large public accounting firm in the Midwest. While growing up, she watched her dad succeed in his business career, which inspired her to major in business in college. During Beth's freshman year, she took many introductory business courses and found that she really enjoyed accounting. Through talking to older classmates, she discovered that an accounting major could open many other career doors in the business world.

Recognizing that her course work would be important when she started looking for a job in accounting, Beth set out to get a solid background in accounting. She began with basic accounting classes, including managerial accounting and financial accounting. Then Beth narrowed her studies to cost accounting, tax, and law. Since computers now play an important role in accounting, Beth also took a few computer courses. One course was focused entirely on learning how to design and use spreadsheets to organize and analyze financial data.

In preparing for a career in accounting, Beth believes that it is necessary to acquire good communication, writing, and analytical skills. She recommends getting started in an accounting career by taking an internship that will give you a bird's-eye view of what the responsibilities of accountants are in the workplace. An internship will also let you use the skills gained in your course work and see how all the areas of accounting fit together. Furthermore, internships provide solid professional contacts and often lead to jobs. Even if you are as well prepared as Beth was for this profession, you are likely to receive some formal on-the-job training when you take your first position.

Working in Public Accounting

Public accountants work for public accounting firms or have their own businesses. The largest public accounting firms are now known as the Big Five: Arthur Andersen, Ernst & Young, KPMG, Deloitte Touche Tohmatsu International, and Price Waterhouse Coopers. These companies dominate accounting throughout the world. They have garnered the business of large and medium-size companies that issue publicly traded securities and employ thousands of accountants. Of course, there are many opportunities for accountants to work in midsize firms and small firms with just a few accountants. At these smaller firms or your own accounting office, you are not likely to work on accounts of major global businesses.

In many public accounting firms, especially smaller ones, work revolves around tax matters, such as preparing business or individual income tax returns or advising companies of the tax advantages and disadvantages of certain business decisions. Some public accountants concentrate more on the consulting side of accounting, which involves offering advice to businesses on such matters as compensation, employee health care benefits, the design of accounting and data processing systems, and controls to safeguard assets. Others choose to specialize in forensic accounting, which entails investigating and interpreting bankruptcies and other complex financial transactions. Still, there are others who work primarily in auditing, examining financial statements and reporting to investors and authorities whether they have been prepared and reported correctly. Public accountants also serve as liaisons with lenders, help with estate planning, give advice on personal financial planning, install efficient accounting systems, and maintain accounting records.

A Day in the Life of a Public Accountant

Malana Sanders has been a public accountant for almost two years. During this time, she has found her busy workdays are full of new tasks, new clients, and new areas of accounting. She is always learning.

Whether Malana is working in her office or at a client's home or business, her day usually begins around 8:30 A.M. Her to-do list is almost always long and varied. If Malana is in the office, she usually spends the time completing audit documentation. She also meets with her supervisor to discuss the results of an audit. She may even present her documentation to her supervisor. Depending on the size of an audit, Malana may work alone or as part of a team. She also works on financial statement reports or legal reports. If she is outside of the office, she may find herself helping conduct an audit at a warehouse or presenting her financial conclusions about an organization at a corporation meeting with upper management. No matter where she is, this financial maven is always dealing with money matters.

Malana has learned that organization is very important in her job. She also says that accountants must be able to handle several tasks at one time and stay calm while shifting from task to task. Being able to prioritize helps Malana complete all the tasks on her agenda.

Malana usually works approximately fifty-hour weeks. This may vary when she travels to client sites or works to complete an audit. She may also work on Saturdays when conducting audits or trying to meet a deadline.

An Accountant with a Big Five Firm

Mary Maxfield is currently an accountant with a Big Five firm. One of Mary's most important jobs is gathering an organization's financial data to analyze and interpret it for the organization's management. She prepares three major levels of financial statements: compilations, reviews, and audits. Each statement provides different information and is intended for different uses and users. Mary gathers this information in many ways. She usually starts with the compilation statement, which involves looking through financial statements such as balance sheets and related income and cash flow statements put out by the organization. While this gives Mary a great deal of information, it does not tell her all she needs to know. For more information, Mary starts the review, which requires some investigation to complete. She frequently travels to the location of the organization and interview personnel. Not only must Mary learn about the current financial condition of the organization, she must also learn to understand the organization's business before completing her review. The final step is the audit, which consists of tests of documentary evidence supporting the transactions recorded in the organization's books. She verifies the physical existence of inventories and confirms the assets and liabilities of the organization through correspondence with customers, creditors, attorneys, and banks. Once this step is completed, Mary puts together documentation explaining her research and renders an opinion on the organization's financial statements.

Take a look at Mary's resume to see the type of background that these firms are seeking.

MARY MAXFIELD

OBJECTIVE

Desire a position with medium to large public accounting firm in the audit, tax, or consulting function. Interested in expanding on my communication, leadership, and accounting skills through the continual professional education gained on client assignments. Aspire to obtain greater responsibilities in the firm.

EDUCATION
Indiana University, Bloomington, IN
Bachelor of Science, December 1995, Accounting, Major GPA: 3.5, Overall GPA: 3.5

EXPERIENCE
Elder-Beerman Department Stores, Lancaster, OH
Sales Clerk 05/91–01/95 (seasonal employment)
Operated terminals efficiently, assisted customers, and helped change displays. Handled several jobs in a variety of departments as needed.

Walt Disney World Company, Lake Buena Vista, FL
College Program, Sales Hostess 01/93–05/93
Nationally selected from over 200 colleges and universities to be a participant in the living, working, and learning experience of the Walt Disney World College Program. Responsibilities included providing quality guest service to over 100,000 guests, contributing to the efficiency of retail transactions, and managing hands-on interaction with people from all over the world. Attended ten business seminars (30 hours) designed to teach management philosophies of Disney World Company and lived in a multicultural student environment. Gained leadership ability through informal opportunities to train cast members.

Musical Arts Center, Bloomington, IN
Stage Crew 02/92–05/92, 08/92–12/92
Assisted in the construction of sets for university operas. Responsible for behind-the-scenes duties during rehearsals and performances. Worked up to 30 hours during rehearsal weeks while a full-time student.

ACTIVITIES AND HONORS
Dean's List: achieved three semesters.
Delta Sigma Pi: professional business fraternity. *Social Chairperson* (Fall '93), responsible for budgeting and coordinating a pledge class dance. *Secretary* (Fall '94), responsible for preparing and maintaining a spreadsheet of membership records for 90 members as well as the documentation of weekly chapter meetings. *Senior Vice President* (Fall '95), organized and coordinated several recruiting events for the fraternity.
Delta Sigma Pi Summer Leadership Academy (Summer '94). Chosen to participate in the first annual weekend of seminars emphasizing the development of leadership skills in fraternity offices and the profession.
Beta Alpha Psi, national accounting fraternity (pledged Spring '95). Attained Gold Active membership status. Newsletter Committee.

Working in Management Accounting

Management accountants work for companies from the giant General Motors to small companies with only a few employees. They are also known as industrial, corporate, or private accountants. If you choose this field of accounting, you will record and analyze the financial information of the company where you work. You will provide information to assist company managers in planning, evaluating, and controlling the operations of the business. You will write reports that are specifically tailored to support the types of decisions that are being made in the organization. You may also prepare financial reports for nonmanagement groups, including stockholders, creditors, regulatory agencies, and tax authorities. Within a business you will work with many different areas, including the accounting department, financial analysis, planning and budgeting, and cost accounting.

A Corporate Financial Accountant

Becky Seffernick works as a credit manager in the financial accounting department of a large industrial corporation. She traces her career start back to an AP accounting class in high school where she quickly picked up accounting principles. While college classes gave her almost all the on-the-job skills she needed, she did have to learn the business of the corporation and how they operated internally.

In her current job, Becky has to handle a variety of tasks. She spends 50 percent of her time at a desk putting together budgets, financial reports, and financial statements. The rest of her time is spent in meetings with customers and management. Some travel is involved in her job as she visits customers to learn about their businesses. Her busiest time is the end of the month. With nine divisions to control, it takes considerable time to consolidate all the accounting statements and balance them. Once this is done, Becky generates monthly reports that are distributed to upper managers in the corporation.

Career Advice

Becky feels that it is extremely important to have good people skills in management accounting. And she believe that internships and classes in public speaking are definitely helpful in preparing for this career.

Working in Government Accounting

Accountants employed by federal, state, and local governments see that revenues are received and expenditures are made in accordance with laws and regulations. Government accountants and auditors maintain and examine the records of government agencies and audit private businesses and individuals whose activities are subject to government regulations or taxation. Many government accountants work for the federal government as Internal Revenue Service agents. Others work with the Securities and Exchange Commission, the General Accounting Office, and the armed forces. Wherever there is a governmental unit involved with the collection or disbursement of money, there are government accountants. There are also jobs in financial management, financial institution examination, and budget analysis and administration.

The unique characteristics, objectives, and constituents of government organizations necessitate a financial reporting system that differs in several ways from that developed for private enterprises. In this area, decisions are evaluated in light of social and political objectives and constraints. As a result, government accountants focus on the acquisition and use made of financial resources and on compliance with legal requirements and restrictions.

The Professional Path of a Government Accountant

While Peter Goodwin was in college, he worked part-time in the accounting department of a large moving company doing posting and balance sheets. Before graduation, the senior accountant became ill and Peter assumed his responsibilities. He stayed with the firm for several years and became assistant treasurer. Personal computers were just coming on the scene, and Peter, recognizing the growing role that computers would play in the accounting profession, went back to school to get a degree in computer technology.

After graduation, Peter applied for a government job with the Department of the Army and obtained a job in financial operations. He began at a slightly higher level than most accountants because of prior military experience and his accounting background. As a GS-9, he worked in foreign military sales doing reconciliations on various government contracts with different countries. After a year, he became a GS-11.

Peter applied for his next position as a systems accountant and became a GS-12. In this job, he used his computer training and accounting background to develop computer applications that would allow employees to go from manual processing to automated accounting. He received a reward for eliminating the need to make manual corrections of errors as well as employee overtime in this area.

His next move was to the expenditure division, where he was responsible for scheduling all computer jobs and continued to develop new computer applications. Peter became a supervisor in this area. Then he was selected to be part of a pilot study using the total quality management approach. His efforts were so successful that he was chosen for a GS-13 position in charge of treasury reporting. Today, he is a team leader of a combined developmental team of programmers and accountants who are developing a data warehouse environment for future accounting systems.

According to Peter, the difference between government and other accounting jobs is that you are not concerned with profits. Also, what you do is based on the moneys appropriated by Congress and by the legislation passed by Congress. Peter plans to continue working as a government accountant and is proud of the work he has done to make it more efficient.

Internal Auditing

Auditing is increasingly important in the field of accounting because of recent government concern about financial accountability, fraudulent financial reporting, and business ethics. The domain of auditing can be divided into two areas: external auditing and internal auditing. External auditors do not work for organizations but are concerned with attesting to the fairness of the presentation of an organization's financial statements. Internal auditors work for an organization and have the responsibility of examining and evaluating their organizations' financial and information systems, management procedures, and internal controls to ensure that records are accurate and controls are adequate. They also review an organization's operations by evaluating its efficiency, effectiveness, and compliance with corporate policies and procedures, laws, and government regulations.

Internal auditors are considered management's right arm because they evaluate the quality of the organization's performance. While employers may look for internal auditors with accounting degrees, other degrees in related fields are acceptable. There are many types of highly specialized auditors, such as health care auditors, bank auditors, legal auditors, electronic data processing auditors, environmental auditors, and engineering auditors.

An Internal Auditor

Philip Ramon is a results-driven team player who possesses a consistent record of business success in a number of different assignments. His background includes a bachelor's degree in marketing and an M.B.A. with an emphasis in finance. He is also a CPA. While attending school, Philip worked for a large multimedia corporation in California; he has stayed with this company for the past seventeen years.

His first job upon completion of his undergraduate degree was as the supervisor of a call center. While there, Philip managed a group of service representatives who answered phones and handled customers' requests. After one year in this group, Philip was promoted to the new product analysis department as the senior financial analyst. In this role, he conducted the financial analysis of potential new products. He created forecasts and financial and economic spreadsheets and prepared reports for upper management. Philip was also responsible for filing financial tariffs with the government.

The Career Path for an Internal Auditor

After a two-year spell on the sales side of the business as a sales manager, Philip became a senior internal auditor. In his new position, he performed all phases of financial, operational, and compliance audits. Before starting a new audit, he established the audit's objectives and the scope of work, came up with an estimated budget, performed a preliminary survey, and then conducted the audit. Upon completion of the audit, Philip gathered his team's information and wrote a detailed report of needed improvements and recommendations for how to fix problems; he made formal presentations to the group audited and to senior management. After hearing the presentation and reading the report, the group that was audited was given a few weeks to respond to and fix items listed in the audit. Finally, sometimes up to a year after the audit began, Philip was once again asked to review the group's procedures to make sure it now would pass his audit.

Career Advice

Philip suggests that if you want to enter the world of finance, you should be prepared to work long hours. He typically works eight to ten hours a day.

What It Takes to Become an Accounting Professional

Most accounting firms, businesses, and organizations seeking accountants and internal auditors are looking for individuals who have at least a bachelor's degree in accounting or a related major for all entry-level positions. Some employers prefer job candidates to have a master's degree in accounting or in business administration with a concentration in accounting. For beginning accounting and auditing positions in the federal government, four years of college (including twenty-four semester hours in accounting or auditing) or an equivalent combination of education and experience is required. Most employers are now looking for employees who are familiar with computers and their applications in accounting and internal auditing. In this profession, as in so many others, previous experience in accounting or auditing can help you get a job. Many colleges offer students an opportunity to gain this experience through summer or part-time internship programs conducted by public accounting or business firms.

When you enter this profession, you must be prepared to keep up with changes in laws and accounting practices, meet certification requirements, and strive to advance professionally. There are many ways that these goals can be accomplished. Many employers and professional associations offer seminars and courses, as do colleges and universities.

Professional Certification and Licensing

Once you are in the job market, professional recognition through certification or licensure provides you with a distinct advantage. While there are many types of prestigious certifications and licenses that an accountant can receive, one of the best known is the Certified Public Accountant (CPA) credential. To get this certification, which is issued by states, you must meet certain basic requirements. In most states, you need to complete 150 semester hours of course work, which is 30 credit hours more than the typical four-year bachelor's degree in accounting. You also need to pass the rigorous Uniform CPA Examination. All states use this four-part examination, which requires two days of testing and months of studying and preparing. Each year only about one-quarter of those who take this test pass. It is a good idea to take extra courses during your early college years, as well as summer school courses, so you can leave your last semester free for a cram course to focus on and review the four years of general and accounting education courses that you have taken in college before tackling the CPA exam. In addition, before getting the designation CPA, most states will require you to have some accounting experience. And to renew your license, you will need to take continuing professional education courses.

Recognition from Professional Societies

It is becoming more important for those in the accounting profession to have certification from a professional society. This certification based on examinations, previous and continuing course work, and experience indicates that a level of professional competence has been reached in a specialized field of accounting and auditing. For example, an accountant who chooses to specialize in tax accounting may take examinations to become an Accredited Tax Preparer (ATP) or Accredited Tax Advisor (ATA). These are professional credentials issued by the Accreditation Council for Accountancy and Taxation (ACAT). In order to receive these credentials, you must complete a prescribed program of study and examination specified by the National Endowment for Financial Education. Other professional society certifications include the Certified Management Accountant (CMA), the Certified Internal Auditor (CIA), and the Certified Information Systems Auditor (CISA).

Climbing the Career Ladder

The ultimate reward for all work is career growth and personal satisfaction. Capable accountants and auditors are able to advance rapidly, while those with inadequate academic preparation may be assigned routine jobs and find promotion difficult. Graduates of community colleges and business and correspondence schools as well as bookkeepers and accounting clerks can obtain junior accounting positions and advance to more responsible positions by demonstrating their accounting skills on the job.

Most beginning public accountants start by assisting with work for several clients. In this field, you will usually advance within one to two years to a job with more responsibilities and experience and to senior positions within another few years. Outstanding public accountants may become supervisors, managers, or partners; open their own firms; or transfer to executive positions in management accounting or internal auditing in private firms.

As a management accountant, you will probably start as a cost accountant, staff accountant, junior internal auditor, or trainee for another accounting position. After a few years experience, you can expect to advance to accounting manager, chief cost accountant, budget director, or manager of internal auditing. Some management accountants even become controllers, treasurers, financial vice presidents, chief financial officers, or corporation presidents. If you begin as an entry-level accountant with the federal government, you can expect to be promoted within two years.

Within the field of accounting, there is a large degree of mobility among public accountants, management accountants, and internal auditors, which allows them to advance their careers. Many accounting professionals shift into management accounting or internal auditing from public accounting, or between internal auditing and management accounting. It is not as common for accountants and auditors to move from either management accounting or internal auditing into public accounting.

Pathway to Success as a Management Accountant

Allen Martin started his accounting career at a small public accounting firm where he had the opportunity to work with many types of clients from construction companies to credit firms. He really enjoyed learning about all the various types of businesses; however, he found that he most enjoyed working with manufacturing firms. When he was offered a job from a manufacturer where he had helped perform audits, he took a position with the firm and has been there for fifteen years. Allen started with the firm as a staff accountant. Because of his prior work experience he quickly moved into the position of an assistant controller and then to his present job as controller.

Looking at the Future— Employment Trends

Currently, there are more than one million accountants and auditors in the United States—20 percent are CPAs and 12 percent are CIAs. And the future is bright for these accounting professionals. As long as the economy continues to grow, the number of business establishments will increase, requiring more accountants and auditors to set up their books, prepare their taxes, and provide management advice. Furthermore, new roles are now emerging for accountants and auditors as they assume an even greater management advisory role and expand their consulting services. This will further increase the demand for public and management accountants in the coming years.

Today, companies and organizations are offering more perks (bonuses, moving expenses, flexible work schedules, and stock options) than ever before as they seek to retain existing employees and hire new ones. Demand is especially high for CPAs and those who hold advanced accounting degrees. With international trade growing, experts in international accounting are currently in high demand. The need is also high for internal auditors as organizations seek ways to become more efficient. Students with the appropriate credentials in accounting are being actively recruited on college campuses across the country. As long as the economy remains robust, the demand for accounting professionals will remain high.

Salaries

A shortage of accounting professionals in public accounting firms has led to an increase in salaries in all areas of accounting. Salaries for accountants and auditors vary greatly depending on the employee's educational background, work experience, and certifications or licenses. The following chart shows the current range of salaries for accountants in different fields of accounting. Accounting professionals working in small firms will typically earn less than those working in medium or large firms.

Accountants' Salaries (median)

Public Accounting

1–3 years	$33,400–42,000
3–5 years	$42,000–50,000
Managers	$48,500–62,000

Auditors

1–3 years	$25,000–39,400
3–5 years	$27,000–46,600
Senior Auditors	$34,300–57,800
Managers	$40,000–81,900

Government Accounting

1–3 years	$19,500–27,000
3–5 years	$29,000–48,000
Managers	$48,000–58,000

More Career Information

For more information regarding careers in accounting, the CPA standards and examinations, college scholarships, and internships, contact any of the following sources:

American Institute of Certified Public Accountants
Harborside Financial Center
201 Plaza III
Jersey City, NJ 07311-3881

Institute of Management Accountants
10 Paragon Dr.
Montvale, NJ 07645-1760

National Society of Public Accountants and the Accreditation
Council for Accountancy and Taxation
1010 North Fairfax St.
Alexandra, VA 22314

The Institute of Internal Auditors
249 Maitland Ave.
Altamonte Springs, FL 32701

For information on accredited accounting programs and educational institutions offering a specialization in accounting or business management, contact:

American Assembly of Collegiate Schools of Business
605 Old Ballas Rd., Suite 220
St. Louis, MO 63141

CHAPTER THREE

Helping People Buy and Sell Stocks

The Job of Securities Sales Representatives

*I*f you want to buy or sell a few shares of Microsoft, General Motors, or Sears Roebuck stock, you would most likely use the services of a securities sales representative, more commonly known as a stockbroker. This individual would relay your order through his or her firm's offices to the floor of a securities exchange, such as the New York Stock Exchange, or to the firm's trading department so the transaction could be completed. Thousands of these transactions take place each day in large brokerage houses, such as Merrill Lynch, Salomon Smith Barney, and Paine Webber, which have branches across the country. They also take place in much smaller regional and local brokerage houses. Besides being called stockbrokers, securities sales representatives are known as registered representatives and account executives. They are the financial mavens who help us invest our money.

The Many Jobs of Securities Sales Representatives

Buying and selling stock is certainly not the only job of securities sales representatives. They will help their customers buy and sell bonds, shares in mutual funds, insurance annuities, and other financial products. They also provide many other related services for their customers. Depending on a customer's knowledge of the market, they may explain the meaning of stock market terms and trading practices, offer financial counseling, or devise an individual financial portfolio for the client, including securities, life insurance, corporate and municipal bonds, mutual funds, certificates of deposit, annuities, and other investments. They may also offer advice on the purchase or sale of particular securities. The relationship between you (the investor) and your security representative is typically close and confidential. Once your security representative understands your needs, you will be able to transact all of your trading over the phone.

Not all customers have the same investment goals. Some individuals may prefer long-term investments designed either for capital growth or to provide income over the years; others might want to invest in speculative securities that they hope will rise in price quickly.

Securities sales representatives furnish information about the advantages and disadvantages of an investment based on each person's objectives. They also supply the latest price quotations on any security in which the investor is interested, as well as information on the activities and financial positions of the corporations issuing these securities. This is a great job for money movers who wish to spend every minute of their workday trying to help others make money.

You do need to know that much of the time of beginning sales representatives may not be spent in financial activities but in finding clients and building a client base. Most rely heavily on phone solicitation. They also find clients through business and social contacts. At times, they can inherit clients from representatives who have retired or moved to other jobs.

A Quick Look at the Workplace

There is a great deal of activity in the brokerage and investment houses where securities sales representatives work. When sales activity increases, due perhaps to unanticipated changes in the economy, the pace may become very hectic. It is decidedly not a quiet place to work, with representatives talking on the phone and tapping on the keys of the computers that continually provide them with information on the prices of securities. If you choose this career, you could find a job in any part of the country. However, most representatives work in large cities.

A Young Stockbroker

Ben Mitchell is a go-getter in the brokerage world. He is a twenty-five-year-old account executive in the Tampa, Florida, office of Dean Witter Reynolds. At his company and other large brokerage firms, the securities sales force is typically composed of individuals who are college educated and several years out of school. Ben fits this pattern. After graduating from college with a major in history and a minor in business, he worked for a mortgage and then an insurance company. When his father became ill, he decided to pursue a higher wage earning career and chose the brokerage industry. Nearing the completion of his first year with Dean Witter Reynolds, Ben is earning virtually the same amount he did previously; however, he knows that the brokerage industry can yield a substantially higher income over the lifetime of his career.

Ben's typical workday begins at the office no later than 7:30 in the morning. He starts his day by reading the *Wall Street Journal* to check the value of stocks in which he is interested and to get a feel of what the stock market is doing. Ben spends the rest of his day researching clients' accounts and trying to contact as many people as he can. He starts hitting the phones, "cold calling like a fool," and tries to recruit clients all day. As Ben explains, "The more people you speak to, the greater chance you have of establishing a relationship."

Almost every brokerage firm's securities sales employees are paid on a commission basis. It can be great to have an unlimited earning potential, but that doesn't mean it is going to happen overnight. At this point in his career, Ben finds that more often than not, he will work all day and leave with nothing to show for it.

The Pluses and Minuses

The most gratifying thing that Ben does as a stockbroker is to help people obtain their desired financial goals through his knowledge and hard work. Ben achieves this by getting to know as much about the client as he can. He works at developing an interpersonal relationship so the clients will turn to him for all financial advice. He knows that he has done a good job when clients call to ask what kind of car they should buy instead of focusing on what they can afford.

One downside or difficult aspect of Ben's job is that he must be able to differentiate between making a decision with his heart and making a well-researched decision. About his profession, Ben says that if you can't come to terms with the fact that clients will lose money with you more often than they make it, you will have an ulcer. Ben believes that as long as his customers have a balanced portfolio they will come out ahead, as diversification is really the key to investing. With a wide variety of securities, one facet of a client's portfolio will always outperform the other through any market cycle. Another downside for a securities sales representative is realizing that people are not just going to walk in the door and give you their life savings. You need to earn their trust and respect and then hope the money will follow.

Future Plans

Ben plans to stay with his current firm for several more years, although he believes the future holds many positions with other companies. At some point in his career, he would like to start his own business. In the brokerage industry, many people move around between firms until they find the right fit, as firms are quite different.

Career Advice

If you make the decision to become a securities sales representative like Ben, you should be prepared for a lot of hard work and long hours. It is also important to be honest in your dealings with clients, as they will appreciate your integrity. Ben says that a good career guidepost is to always look after your clients' interests as if they were your own.

Job Qualifications

While employers, especially the larger brokerage houses, want securities sales representatives who have a college degree, your major is not important. You could have a degree in anything from business to history to music. You will, however, find it helpful to have taken courses in business administration, economics, and finance because prospective employers want you to be well informed about economic trends and conditions.

Many employers consider your personal qualities and skills more important than your academic background. They want employees who have sales ability and good communications skills, are well groomed, and have a strong desire to succeed. You will also need to have self-confidence in order to handle the frequent rejections that are part of this job. Because maturity and the ability to work independently are important, many employers prefer to hire those individuals who have achieved success in other jobs. Some firms prefer candidates with sales experience, particularly those who have worked on commission in areas such as real estate or insurance. Therefore, most entrants to this occupation transfer from other jobs.

Licensing Requirements

To become a securities sales representatives, you must meet state licensing requirements, which generally include passing an examination and, in some cases, furnishing a personal bond. In addition, sales representatives must register as representatives of their firm according to regulations of the securities exchanges where they do business or the National Association of Securities Dealers (NASD). Before beginners can qualify as registered representatives, they must pass the General Securities Registered Representative Examination administered by the NASD. They must also be an employee of a registered firm for at least four months. Most states require a second examination—the Uniform Securities Agents State Law Examination. These tests measure the prospective representative's knowledge of the securities business, customer protection requirements, and record-keeping procedures. Many people take correspondence courses in preparation for the securities examinations.

States that do not require brokers to obtain a license empower the state's attorney general to act against illegal practices. The government has laws that regulate securities dealers at both the federal and state levels. Nearly all states have a Sales of Securities Act created to protect investors from fraudulent practices in the sale of securities. It is important to have knowledge of the laws in order to avoid violating them.

Training

When you take a job as a securities sales representative, your employer will probably provide on-the-job training to help you meet the requirements for registration. In most firms, this training period generally takes about four months. If you are a trainee at a large firm, you may receive classroom instruction in securities analysis, effective speaking, and the finer points of selling; take courses offered by business schools and associations; and undergo a period of on-the-job training lasting up to two years. Many firms like to rotate their trainees among various departments in the firm to give them a broader perspective of the securities business. In small firms, sales representative generally receive training at outside institutions and on the job.

Securities sales representatives must understand the basic characteristics of a wide variety of financial products offered by brokerage firms. Representatives periodically take training, through their firms or outside institutions, to keep abreast of new financial products as they are introduced on the market and to improve their sales techniques. Training in the use of computers is becoming more and more important as the securities sales business is increasingly automated.

A Look at Advancement Opportunities

The principal form of advancement for securities sales representatives is an increase in the number and size of the accounts they handle. Although beginners usually service the accounts of individual investors, eventually they may handle very large institutional accounts such as those of banks and pension funds. Some experienced sale representative become branch office managers and supervise other sales representatives while continuing to provide services for their own customers. A few representatives advance to top management positions or become partners in their firms.

The Story of a Successful Vice President

As the vice president and resident manager of a brokerage office in Northern California, Noel Sherry has what can be considered one of the most difficult jobs at Merrill Lynch. In this position, Noel wears two distinct hats. One is that of financial consultant, a role that demands he acquire clients, design financial plans, structure portfolios, and dispense financial advice. In addition, he must also keep abreast of changing markets and all the news that may impact those markets. The greatest challenge of being a financial consultant is to make money for clients in markets over which he has no control. The competition is fierce as many firms are vying for the same customer's investment dollar. The pressure is enormous. Clients have big expectations both in terms of performance and service.

The other hat Noel wears is that of the resident manager, requiring him to manage the office. In this role, Noel is surrounded by intelligent, high-achieving, hard-working individuals. At Merrill Lynch, all financial consultants must have a college degree and almost always have a resume that reflects unusual patterns of success in various areas of their lives. As manager, Noel is in charge of all office personnel, hiring, firing, etc. He also attends to all human resources issues, serves as an ambassador to the community, deals with client issues, and runs the office profitably and in accordance with the firm's objectives. Handling both roles translates into an incredibly busy and demanding job with a workday that usually runs ten to twelve hours.

While this is a difficult and demanding industry in which to work, it can be an extremely rewarding one if you have the drive and desire to be successful. Noel began working as a financial consultant in 1982, right after graduating from the University of California at Berkeley. While he has continued working as a financial consultant, he has also taken on the roles of sales manager in the San Jose office, founder and manager of the office in Capitola, and is now the manager in Mill Valley. Noel believes that his future holds the possibility of a full-time management position in an even larger metropolitan Merrill Lynch office.

Career Advice

Noel points out that contacts internal to the company you want to work for can help you land your dream job. However, he points out that it is even more important to have a resume that reflects your drive and motivation for high achievement. Once your resume is in top shape and you get that job, you will have to learn how to do it successfully. According to Noel, nothing, even training and classes, is as beneficial as what you learn while actually working on the job.

He recommends that anyone who is interested in being employed as a securities sales representative, start his or her career by working for a large firm. A larger company will typically have a greater number of clients, be able to offer a more comprehensive list of services, and possess a well-known and reliable reputation. In the larger firms, entry-level security sales representatives are often called associate financial consultants for at least their first two years on the job. During this time, you will concentrate on learning the business and building your clientele. Some firms will provide you with a mentor, someone who has prior successful work experience, to serve as your guide.

One other snippet of information that you need to know is that your work hours are tied to the hours of the New York Stock Exchange. So if you are working on the West Coast, your day will start at 6:30 A.M. to coincide with the 9:30 opening of the exchange in New York. Furthermore, your day often won't conclude until 4:00 or 5:00 in the afternoon.

Other Financial Services Opportunities

It is important to understand that securities sales representatives are not the only employees working in brokerage houses. In large brokerage houses, there are many other people involved in helping clients manage their money. Portfolio managers concentrate on helping clients maintain a portfolio of investments, while other employees concentrate on securities research, investment strategies, and managing the day-to-day operation of the firm. There are also accountants keeping track of all the investments. In small brokerage firms, an individual will typically have more than one responsibility.

Working as a Portfolio Manager

Robert Tredway works for Lawson Kroeker, a small investment management company in Omaha, Nebraska, with just five employees. He is a portfolio manager who assists individuals in the development of their portfolios and financial goals. Robert thrives on individual, one-on-one contact with his clients and chooses to emphasize the service and personal aspects of his job.

After obtaining his undergraduate degree in agricultural science and then his M.B.A., Robert went to work for an Omaha bank as a fixed-income analyst working with the buying, selling, and tracking of bonds. In addition, he was asked to serve in a support position to oversee the management of minor portfolios. Robert says that individuals starting out in this industry can expect to crunch a lot of numbers, and they should know a great deal about current technology because they will use the computer for financial analysis and client contact. It might also be necessary for them to utilize the firm's computer system to surf the Web for information.

After working for the bank, Robert moved to a governmental agency as a finance manager, a position that he didn't like as it lacked contact with clients. He had two more positions in large companies and banks before he started working at his present firm. This career move reduced the number of his clients from four hundred to approximately forty, a change that has enabled him to spend far more time building relationships with his clients and managing each of their portfolios. Another change in moving from a large firm to a small one was that he stopped receiving a straight salary and company benefits and began to be compensated based on the company's profitablility.

Career Advice

In order to be a successful portfolio manager, Robert says that you must enjoy working with people and realize that you are responsible for one of their most important possessions—money. If you are shy and reluctant to work with people, you could still be in this business by electing to manage a mutual fund in which you deal only with your staff and rarely if ever meet individual investors.

Working as an Investment Strategist

Darren Clauws became the chief investment strategist for the High Street Financial Group after working for the company a mere two years. Right after completing his M.B.A., Darren started at the firm as an analyst responsible for supporting his manager with portfolio accounting and security research. Because Darren got his foot in the door with a small, relatively new, and rapidly growing company, and because he is a very hard worker, he was quickly promoted to his current position and more than doubled his salary.

Darren's job responsibilities include portfolio accounting, security research and selection, economic research, and continual reevaluation of the company's investment strategy. He also speaks with clients to keep them abreast of market trends and High

Street's investment strategy for the future. Portfolio accounting involves keeping all client records up-to-date. Without accurate records one could erroneously buy a security the client already has or worse, sell a security that the client doesn't own. Record keeping involves downloading client transactions every morning from the custodian's mainframe computer and reconciling the changes with his company's records. It is like balancing two hundred checkbooks every day.

Security research and selection, economic research, and reevaluating the firm's strategy takes up the bulk of Darren's day. While the stock exchanges are open, Darren continually tracks news releases on the economy as well as companies in which his firm's clients own stock and stock he is interested in purchasing for clients' portfolios. Periodically, clients call to receive updates on their accounts and to discover where High Street is looking to invest in the future.

Darren also works closely with the operations manager, who is responsible for opening accounts for new clients, transferring client assets, and making sure clients have completed all of their paperwork correctly. It is important for Darren to know when clients are depositing money or transferring assets so that he can watch for the money to hit their accounts and thus become new assets for him to manage.

Darren works an average of forty-five to fifty-five hours per week. At times, he needs to work on weekends to get caught up on research, and he is always bringing analyst reports, annual reports, and corporate briefs home to read in the evenings.

The most enjoyable aspect of Darren's job is knowing when he has done a good job. He is easily able to measure his success by matching his results with his clients' expectations. These expectations may involve simply outperforming what the client could have earned on a money market (interest bearing) cash account or the more challenging task of outperforming the market indices. Unfortunately, these same expectations can also be disadvantages.

The clients know exactly when you are not doing your job well, and this is where the stress of this job arises. One of the best ways to combat this is to manage the clients' expectations.

Darren tries to sell his company to prospective clients by gaining their trust and keeping in touch with them on a regular basis. There is nothing more important in the investment industry, he says, than making sure your clients can trust you to manage their money. In many cases, Darren is managing all the money that his clients have saved during their lives. This is an awesome responsibility, as clients count on that money for retirement or to make significant purchases such as homes.

Career Advice

Darren believes that as the American workforce continues to become more educated, it will become increasingly important for those in the investment industry to have not only a bachelor's degree but also a graduate degree in order to differentiate themselves from their peers. He also recommends becoming a Certified Financial Analyst (CFA), which is the most prestigious designation a person in this career can achieve. It is considered equal to attaining a graduate degree in economics and finance from a top-tier business school, and he recommends it highly for people entering the buy-side of the investment industry. *Buy-side* is a term used to describe analysts, economists, and other back-office research positions in the industry. The sell-side of this industry is made up of the brokers, account executives, and salespeople who generate the clientele.

In addition to taking the obvious courses in economics and finance, Darren recommends gaining experience in the information systems area. Since technology in this industry is growing exponentially, he believes that without extensive knowledge of computers and the more popular software packages, a person cannot succeed in this career.

A Look at What Securities Sales Representatives Earn

Trainees usually are paid a salary and lower commission rate until they meet licensing and registration requirements. After they are licensed, registered, and have gained experience, their earnings depend on commissions from the sale or purchase of stocks and bonds or other securities for customers. Commission earnings are likely to be high when there is much buying and selling and lower when there is a slump in market activity. Most firms provide sales representatives with a steady income by paying a "draw against commission"—that is, a minimum salary based on the commissions that they can be expected to earn.

Securities sales representatives who can provide their clients with the most complete financial services enjoy the greatest income stability. Because pay depends on an individual's production, incomes vary wildly, with many representatives earning more than $100,000 a year. Annual incomes can run from $10,000 to $3 million.

Commission Versus Fee-Based Salaries

In 1988 Charles Carnevale and his wife Julie started their own investment firm, EDMP (Earnings Determine Market Price). It is a fee-based firm, which means that its clients pay an annual fee in exchange for the management of their investments. While most companies big and small charge their clients a percentage or commission based on the purchase or sale of a security, Chuck believes that the future of the securities firm is with fee-based portfolio management. Because EDMP's approach is fee based, it will not charge the investor a percentage of each security sale or purchase. Instead, EDMP charges an annual recurring fee of 5 to 10 percent based upon the size of the individual's portfolio—the amount of money they have invested through the company.

Employment Outlook

If you choose to become a securities sales representative, you will find an abundance of jobs because this is a career field that is growing faster than most other occupations. This growth is expected to continue through 2005 as economic growth, rising personal incomes, and greater inherited wealth is increasing the funds available for investment. More individual investors are expected to purchase common stocks, mutual funds, and other financial products after seeking advice from securities sales representatives regarding the increasing array of investment alternatives. Furthermore, representatives now have more financial services to offer as deregulation has enabled brokerage firms to sell certificates of deposit, offer checking and deposit services through cash management accounts, and sell insurance products such as annuities and life insurance.

Growth in the number and size of institutional investors will be strong as more people enroll in pension plans, set up individual retirement accounts, establish trust funds, and contribute to the endowment funds of colleges and other nonprofit institutions. More representatives also will be needed to sell securities issued by new and expanding corporations, by state and local governments financing public improvements, and by foreign governments, whose securities have become attractive to U.S. investors as international trade expands.

Before you choose a career as a securities sales representative, you need to know that the demand for representatives fluctuates as the economy expands and contracts. Thus, in an economic downturn, the number of persons seeking jobs will usually exceed the number of openings—sometimes by a great deal. Even during periods of rapid economic expansion like the United States is experiencing today, competition for securities sales training positions—particularly in larger firms—is keen because of the potentially high earnings.

In searching for a job, you will find job opportunities in large firms are best for mature individuals with successful work experience. Opportunities for inexperienced sales representatives should be greater in smaller firms.

A Look to the Future

With the advancement of technology, the brokerage firm may become a portable unit. Laptops and cell phones will make it possible for securities sales representatives of the future to make a living from home or while on the road. Representatives will be able to sign up new clients and start investing for them right away, trading at any time, day or night. It is even possible that in the more distant future, investors will pick out a lifestyle portfolio and that the majority of an individual's portfolio will be managed by a computer without his or her consent. The representative's role will then be to bring in assets and to constantly sign people up with the firm of record.

CHAPTER FOUR

Buying and Selling Stocks

The Jobs of Traders and Others Who Work with Stocks

S tock exchanges are the market places where traders buy and sell stocks for investors from individuals to huge pension funds. When you tell your securities sales representative that you want to buy or sell a stock, your order is often relayed through the firm's offices to the firm's floor broker or it may be sent directly to a receiving clerk on the floor of the exchange. The environment on the trading floor is absolutely wild. Brokers and traders are yelling, waving their hands, and fighting for prime positions on the floor. As a financial maven, a career as a trader or floor broker should appeal to you because these are jobs that will completely involve you in making financial deals every minute of your workday. They are also very exciting jobs in which transactions worth millions of dollars are completed in just a few seconds.

A Brief History of Stock Exchanges

The New York Stock Exchange is the largest exchange for securities in the world. It was organized in 1792 by twenty-four brokers who met to buy and sell stock under a buttonwood tree on what is now Wall Street in New York City. The New York Stock Exchange isn't the oldest in the country. One year earlier a stock exchange was established in Philadelphia, which was then the leading city in domestic and foreign trade. Nor is the exchange in New York the only one in the United States. Others include the American Stock Exchange, also in New York City, and five regional stock exchanges, which are located in Boston, Cincinnati, Philadelphia, the Midwest, and the Pacific.

The idea of having stock exchanges grew out of early trading activities at trade fairs in Europe during the Middle Ages when traders began using credit and needed supporting documents. During the twelfth century, trading in commercial bills of exchange began in both France and the Low Countries. Later on in 1531, the first European stock exchange similar to today's institutions opened in Antwerp, Belgium. Today, major stock exchanges are located throughout the world in such locations as Tokyo; London; Paris; Montreal; Johannesburg, South Africa; Hong Kong; Singapore; and Milan, Italy.

A Quick Look at Trading Procedures on the Exchange Floor

First of all, you need to envision the scene at the New York Stock Exchange. The setting is similar at other exchanges. Papers litter the floor, the noise volume is horrendous as prices are screamed out to complete transactions, and brokers and traders are dashing around looking for the post where a specific stock is traded. The posts aren't actual posts today, although they once were. Traders, called specialists, are at each post dealing in several stocks that are listed overhead. Inside the post or station, a computer clerk records all transactions. The pandemonium starts when the bell rings at 9:30 A.M. and doesn't end until the final bell at 4:00 P.M. Traders and brokers stay on their feet throughout the day (there are no chairs) and will possibly be able to grab a sandwich for lunch. The action is nonstop.

Trading Procedure

Your trade order is typically received on the floor of the exchange by a clerk of the firm where you placed your order. The clerk passes the order to a broker who goes to the post where the stock is traded and negotiates the purchase or sale of a stock in an auction lasting just seconds. Because this is an auction, stocks are sold to those bidding the highest prices and bought from those offering the lowest prices. It is the specialist (trader) in the stock who keeps the process orderly by buying and selling for his or her own account when there are orders at prices that cannot be executed at once.

The Major Players on the Floor

There are more than thirteen hundred brokers on the trading floor of the New York Stock Exchange. The specialists spend their days within just a few feet of the post where their stocks trade. There are also house brokers who are employed by investment firms such as Merrill Lynch and Smith Barney to execute trades for the firm's clients. They usually stay in one geographic area of the exchange. The independent brokers are self-employed. They handle overflow business from giant firms and work for smaller brokerage houses and large investors. The final players, and the smallest group, are the mixed-business brokers. This group often serves as brokers for regional firms and also trade on behalf of other clients. You will find the same types of brokers at all the exchanges; however, there will be fewer of them because the exchanges are much smaller.

Other Trading Jobs

It is important to understand that not all trading jobs are on the floors of stock exchanges. Brokerage houses, banks, mutual fund companies, investment banks, and other financial institutions also have traders, known as upstairs traders. These traders may handle trades for their firms or customers within the house, with brokers or traders on the floors of exchanges, or with dealers in an over-the-counter market, such as the NASDAQ computerized trading system. Besides the stock market, there are also traders who trade options, commodities, and bonds in a similar fashion.

A Trader on the Pacific Stock Exchange

It is not an easy life to be a trader; however, in this job you are in the center of the financial heartland of America—the stock market. Mark Johnson is on the floor of the Pacific Stock Exchange from 6:30 A.M. to 1:10 P.M. Monday through Friday buying and selling stock options. He works in a pit (a sunken area) with forty to fifty other traders and their clerks. He won't leave the pit until the end of a trading session even to eat lunch because he might miss a trade. Mark buys and sells stock options for approximately twelve stocks. A stock option is a contract conveying a right to buy or sell a stock at a specified price during a specific period of time.

Here's the way an options trade works. With an order in hand, the broker goes to the pit where the option is being traded. The broker begins the trade by loudly asking: "How's the market in (a specific option)?" or "What's the market?" Then Mark and the other traders who deal with that option yell out their prices. The broker then chooses the three traders in one, two, three order who are offering the best price for the customer. If Mark is chosen, he and the broker quickly decide on the size of the trade and Mark gives the broker a ticket. Mark then turns around and hedges his position by buying or selling stock, which he does by yelling out an order to a stock clerk. The action moves at a lightning pace, and Mark could complete a transaction in as little as five seconds.

Behind the Trading Scene

By 5:00 A.M. Mark is in the pit preparing for the opening of the Pacific Stock Exchange, which operates on the same hours as the New York Stock Exchange. The first thing he does is check the clearinghouse records of his trades from the day before to make sure they agree with his tickets. He then checks his current positions to figure out what needs to be adjusted that day. When the market opens, Mark spends the rest of the day making two-sided markets (bids and offers) on the optionable stocks that he deals in. He makes markets based on supply and demand of the public, the current price of the stock, the direction the stock is moving (up or down), and his own position. Mark owns his own seat on the exchange; therefore, how successfully he trades determines entirely how much money he makes. The way he makes money is by taking advantage of the spread between the bid and offer price of options. In other words, to make money he buys options cheaper than he sells them for.

Getting Started as a Trader

While you don't need to be a college graduate to become a trader, you do need to be a whiz at adding and subtracting fractions. Mark became fascinated with trading after taking a college class that involved the hypothetical trading of commodities. He also took a graduate course on option pricing. During this class, a guest lecturer who worked for the Pacific Stock Exchange spoke of career opportunities, and after graduation Mark started at the exchange as a quote operator and really began to learn how to trade. In this job, Mark listened to what was happening in a pit and typed up the bids and offers so the public could see them on a screen and know how options were being priced. Then he learned even more about trading by clerking for a trader for two years. Mark's next step was to use the expertise he had acquired to start trading for himself.

A Trader at an Investment Bank

The trading scene is no less frenetic when it is located at an investment bank. There is just as much yelling out as traders receive and act on orders. One difference is that the traders are sitting down in front of computers that are keeping them constantly up-to-date with what is happening in their market area.

Anthony LeRoy works as a trader at the risk arbitrage desk of a major investment bank in New York City. Prior to becoming a trader, he gained experience in trading operations. His particular job was to catch errors in which the floor report on a stock did not match the report entered into the computer. Today, he has his dream job as a trader. Anthony arrives in the office by 7:00 A.M. and immediately goes on the computer to see if there are any corporate events that can be exploited to earn money for the firm. For example, if one company is purchasing another, it may be advantageous to buy the stock of one company and sell the stock of the other. Sitting behind him are very experienced analysts with whom he will discuss the situation and reach a decision on pricing and when to buy or sell the stocks.

Once the stock market opens, he uses his expertise to decide when to place orders. Anthony has a direct line to his company's floor brokers that he uses hundreds of times a day to call in orders as long as the market is open. His day is spent making trades, consulting with analysts and other traders, and keeping track of what is occurring in the market. At the end of the trading day, he sits back and talks to fellow traders and analysts about the day. They discuss problems and successes and make plans for the next day. It's rather like the sessions coaches hold with their players after every game.

More Trading Jobs

Behind all of the trades that are made on the exchanges, in brokerage houses, and in banks is a small army of brokerage clerks producing records of each trade. Purchase-and-sale clerks match orders to buy with orders to sell. They balance and verify stock trades by comparing the records of the selling firm to those of the buying firm. Dividend clerks ensure that clients receive their payments. Transfer clerks execute customer requests for changes to security registration and examine stock certificates to make sure they adhere to banking regulations. Receive-and-deliver clerks facilitate the receipt and delivery of securities among firms. Margin clerks post accounts and monitor activity in customers' accounts. These jobs in operations are definitely not dead-end jobs and can lead to jobs as traders. Anthony LeRoy, for example, began his financial career in operations.

The Lure of a Career in Trading

There are many challenges in careers associated with the trading of stocks. Decisions have to be made quickly, and they need to be right most of the time for they involve earning or losing money for a client or firm. Financial mavens who are captivated by the actions of the market have a chance to test their expertise every day in predicting which stocks will go up and which will go down in value.

The rewards for being a successful trader are great. In large firms, it is quite easy to earn more than $100,000 a year. House brokers who are on the floor of the New York Stock Exchange can earn from $100,000 to $250,000 in salary and bonuses.

CHAPTER FIVE

Managing Large Amounts of Money

The Job of Portfolio Managers and Other Financial Mavens

B ack about forty years ago, most of the stocks in the United States were owned by individual investors. The Smiths owned some shares in AT&T, while the Johnsons had shares in General Motors. Individual investors still own the majority of shares of stock; however, money has flowed into the market from private pension funds, state and local pension funds, insurance companies, personal trusts, and mutual funds. Some of these groups actually have billions of dollars in the stock market. These large amounts of money are managed by financial mavens called portfolio managers who have the task of deciding which stocks and other financial instruments will be in the portfolios they manage. A small personal trust could have one manager, but a large mutual fund company would have many portfolio managers managing different funds.

Mutual Funds—the New Kid on the Block

The major reason so much money has gone into mutual funds in recent years is that the baby boomers are saving for their retirement. It is decidedly easier to buy shares in a mutual fund than to take the time to research individual stocks or other financial instruments. In addition, mutual funds offer a veritable smorgasbord of choices. If you just want to purchase stocks, there are growth funds, aggressive growth funds, income funds, and international funds, to name just a few of your choices. Mutual funds are not just limited to stocks; there are bond funds, U.S. government income funds, municipal bond funds, precious metals funds, mortgage securities funds, and many other funds. In addition, there are balanced funds that have investments in different combinations of stocks, bonds, and other financial instruments. Investors can choose the fund or funds that meet their interests. Nearly one in three American households today has shares in mutual funds that they have purchased or are in their pension plans at work.

A Portfolio Manager of Three International Funds

Portfolio manager jobs are not limited to mutual fund companies. These jobs are located wherever there are large funds that need to be invested. They are at corporations, unions, government units, colleges, insurance companies, and banks. Laura Fischer is a portfolio manager at a major bank in Chicago, where she manages three international funds. Much of her day on the job is spent gathering information about what is happening in the market, in different companies, and in world economies. She uses electronic sources, newsprint, research analysts, information services, and phone calls to gather the information she needs to make decisions on buying and selling international stocks for the portfolios. Her decisions are also based on whether a fund is gaining or losing money.

Each day Laura spends time talking on the phone and in person to clients who want information about her funds. Most of these clients are large investors. And then in this job, like most others, Laura spends time in meetings that are primarily devoted to gathering and sharing information. She typically attends meetings with company analysts, service information providers, peers, and those who are operationally involved in the buying and selling of shares. Part of Laura's job responsibilities are dictated by federal law. Twice a year, fund managers have to send out information keeping shareholders informed of what is going on in the fund. And when a new fund is started, key information about the fund must be sent out to prospective investors before their money can be accepted.

Laura's Career Path

Laura's background is different from many portfolio managers. She did not major in a business-related field as an undergraduate, but rather in a foreign language, and she does not have an M.B.A. degree. After graduation from college, Laura entered the investment field as a research analyst, which is the first job of most individuals who become portfolio managers. She worked with a senior analyst covering technology stocks. What was so exceptional about this job was that Laura actually gained some portfolio management experience as she was involved not just in making recommendations based on research but in making actual decisions on buying and selling stock. This happened because her boss was an excellent mentor. Two years later, when he moved to another job, Laura got his job and was actually managing a technology fund. For someone to begin managing a fund after two years of experience only happens when great skill in fund management has been demonstrated. Laura, obviously, could apply what she learned through research.

Several years later, Laura began to search for an international job through peer contacts and networking because she wanted to gain firsthand international experience. She was able to join a small British start-up in London, where she managed several funds. Her next career step was to start an office for another British firm in the United States. In this job, she managed the office as well as several funds. The office was so successful that she had to hire more portfolio managers. Laura left this office with several others for work at a small/medium investment company. From this job, she was hired by a large bank that wanted her to devise ways it could secure an international presence in mutual funds. She investigated different ways to do this and ultimately started an international fund. Today, Laura has become a vice president and principal at the bank in charge of international equities. Her department has grown steadily, and she has hired several other portfolio managers to manage different international funds.

More Jobs in Investment Management

You do not have to be a portfolio manager to be involved with the investment of large amounts of money. Behind portfolio managers, there are teams of people supporting the work these managers do. There are research analysts evaluating the performance of different companies, stocks, industries, and economies. Marketing people are needed to sell the funds to the public, companies, and other groups such as pension funds. If you are a money mover who really likes to talk, you may be intrigued with a job as a relationship manager. In this position, you would talk to clients and pass information back and forth between them and the portfolio managers. There are also the traders (described in Chapter 4), who buy and sell stock and other financial instruments for the portfolio managers. If you have a legal background, you could work as a compliance officer making sure that the law was being followed exactly in the sale of funds. There are also many back office administrative jobs handling reports and statements and settling trades. A great number of systems people are needed to work in the following areas: technology, information, trading software, and databases.

A Look at a Few Job Opportunities

The following positions are available at companies selling mutual funds. They will help you understand what employment opportunities exist in the investment arena and the qualifications needed to secure them.

Administrative Assistant

JOB DESCRIPTION:

- Compile information for routine to complex reports and spreadsheets using various software packages

- Assist in implementing office procedures and controls

- Manage human resources administration for group

- Assist in creating presentations, charts, reports and letters

- Handle special business projects as assigned

- Perform various administrative tasks, including answering telephones, referring callers as needed, scheduling appointments, arranging meetings, making copies, distributing mail, making travel arrangements, maintaining supplies and files, and tracking expenses

REQUIRED SKILLS:

- Self-directed individual willing to work overtime

- Excellent PC skills in a Windows environment (including Word, Excel, Power Point, Access, etc.)

- Ability to juggle multiple tasks at one time and remain focused in fast-paced environment

- Capability to work under limited supervision

- High degree of integrity and ability to maintain confidentiality at all times

Research Analyst

JOB DESCRIPTION:

- Work closely with portfolio managers

- Play a vital role in determining the fund's investment performance in an industry

- Interview company managements

- Communicate with research analysts in brokerage community

- Apply economic and industry analysis to the implementation of investment ideas

REQUIRED SKILLS:

- High motivation and intellectual curiosity

- Avid interest in the stock market that has been demonstrated through either previous work or personal investing

- Excellent financial analysis skills

- Good business judgment

Investment Representative

JOB DESCRIPTION:

- Respond to inbound 800-number inquiries and educate potential fund investors to meet their investment objectives

- Perform outbound follow-up contacts to inbound inquiries and actively confirm the client's objectives and close the sale

- Meet or exceed the monthly sales quota through participation in the department's automated inbound/outbound environment

REQUIRED SKILLS:

- Strong sales skills

- Detailed knowledge of mutual fund's products

- Interpersonal skills

- Thorough knowledge of financial industry

- NASD registered with Series 7 and 63 licenses

- One or more years of financial experience

An Arbitrageur at an Investment Bank

Arbitrageurs practice arbitrage, which is the nearly simultaneous purchase and sale of securities in different markets in order to profit from price discrepancies. It also focuses on merger arbitrage when one company is taking over another. This is based on buying one stock and selling the other over a period of three months to a year to make money on the spread in the stock prices. For the past five years, Bill Porter has worked at a major investment bank in New York City as an arbitrageur.

After college, where he majored in economics, Bill went to work at an investment bank as an analyst in mergers and acquisitions. During his third year as an analyst, he was able to secure an apprenticeship in the arbitrage department, which is a very difficult position to get. He began running trading positions as soon as he had acquired sufficient background experience. In this department, you are judged by your success. You could be a great arbitrageur at twenty-four, making more money than a more experienced arbitrageur of forty. Bill devised a very sophisticated trading strategy that has proven so successful he now runs a huge portfolio of the investment bank's own money.

This is not an easy job. Bill leaves home every day by 7:15 A.M. and rarely gets home until twelve hours later. Before the market opens, he is busy researching what has happened the previous day. His research even starts in the taxi taking him to work as he reads the *Wall Street Journal*. Once the market opens, Bill is seated behind his two giant workstation computers looking for spreads that can be turned into profits. When he wants a trade, he yells out to the traders who are sitting down a long table from him. He scarcely stops for lunch in his quest for making money for the firm. When the market closes at 4:00 P.M., he can relax a bit and contemplate the trades he has made that day as well as those he will make in the future, plus he has time to do more research. Bill's success on the job has made him a vice president of the firm before age thirty.

Emerging Job Opportunities

Because mutual funds have met investors' needs so well, they are growing like weeds. At the same time, a number of new services related to these funds have emerged at banks, fund companies, brokerage houses, and new companies. All of this translates into both more jobs and new jobs. Banks and brokerage houses are now selling mutual funds as well as individual stocks. Reams of material have been written on using these funds for retirement and college.

New companies have emerged that track the performance of these funds and write about their quality for investors. In addition, investors can buy CDs and computer programs to keep track of their investments and to learn how to invest their money. Plus, most of the funds have created Web sites on the Internet. All of these new services provide additional job opportunities for those of you who wish to be closely involved with the hottest investment market in recent years. Here is a recent Web ad for an entry-level research position with a financial publisher.

RESEARCH ASSISTANTS: ENTRY-LEVEL POSITIONS   A cutting-edge financial publisher, located in New York City, has immediate openings for research assistants. The ideal candidates must possess an outstanding aptitude for math, superior written and verbal communication skills, the ability to read financial reports and a minimum of two courses in accounting or finance. Familiarity with computers is a plus. Degree preferred.

A Glimpse into the Future

As long as the economy keeps expanding, financial mavens will find a wide variety of jobs wherever there is a large pool of money. Technology will continue to reduce the need for some clerical workers, but at the same time it will increase the need for those with computer expertise. Jobs in this investment sector are highly prized because they pay well and are extremely challenging. Research analysts right out of college can command salaries ranging from $25,000 to $40,000. For a few individuals this will lead to positions as fund managers paying more than $100,000 a year.

CHAPTER SIX

Helping People Manage Their Money

The Job of Financial Planners

N ot too many years ago, money management wasn't too difficult. Today, companies are shifting the responsibility for pensions to individuals through 401(k) plans; the future of social security is uncertain; investing in securities and purchasing insurance require a certain level of expertise; and taxes are complicated. Individuals have to manage their money with skill to provide sufficient funds for a home, education, travel, retirement, and other activities. It is not easy to make financially sound decisions to achieve personal goals. For this reason, many people now look to financial planners for advice about managing their money. In the same way, many companies avail themselves of the services of financial planners.

A Close Look at the Job of Financial Planners

Financial planners are financial mavens who help their clients take financial control of their lives. They use their knowledge of tax and investment strategies, securities, insurance, pension plans, and real estate to develop and implement financial plans that let individuals, couples, and companies realize their financial goals. Financial planners can be generalists who give across-the-board financial advice or specialists limiting their advice to an area such as college planning, debt counseling, or taxes.

There are three distinct roles that financial planners play: investigator, developer, and implementer. During the investigation phase, financial planners spend a great deal of their time interviewing their clients to determine their assets, liabilities, cash flow, insurance coverage, tax status, and financial objectives. The planners also help the clients determine specific financial goals that they wish to achieve. For a family, these goals may be to save money for a new house, establish a college fund for the kids, or to maximize retirement income. For a business, goals may include setting up a benefits plan for employees, reducing taxes, and protecting assets. During this time, the financial planner also helps the client prioritize financial needs: How much risk can be tolerated for certain rewards? Can retirement be delayed to save more money? What comes first, building a college fund or raising the down payment for a new house? At times, the financial manager must serve as a mediator when a couple or business partners do not have the same financial goals.

Depending on the complexity of the client's financial situation and specific goals, this investigative phase can sometimes take months to complete. Once it is completed, the planner then uses all of his or her expertise to analyze the information and develop a financial plan, which may involve consulting outside experts. This phase is not complete until the clients have accepted the plan.

Then it is time to implement the plan. This can involve such things as purchasing securities and insurance, forming trusts, drawing up a budget, consolidating loans, and making wills. The planner may need to have other experts, including securities sales representatives, bankers, and attorneys, help in the implementation of the plan. In a continuing relationship, the financial planner and client will meet from time to time to evaluate and update the plan.

Financial Planners Have Many Workplaces

Many financial planners begin their careers in a sales position at a large financial institution such as a bank or brokerage house. Then after a few years, they often move into the area of financial planning at a large corporation or into one of the steadily growing number of financial advisory firms. Many, however, leave the corporate world to operate as self-employed professionals.

In order to increase the number of clients they have, it is very common for financial planners to teach courses in adult education and community colleges. This introduces them to people who may need their special skills. For the same reason, planners often give speeches to groups, including professional and fraternal organizations. A few financial planners conduct seminars in such areas as investing, taxation, and preparing for retirement, with the idea of increasing their client base.

Starting a Career in Financial Planning

While he was growing up, Bill Whopple knew that he wanted to follow in the footsteps of both his father and grandfather and work in finance, possibly in the family's financial consulting business. In college, he studied finance and took a great number of accounting courses dealing with taxes. To gain more knowledge about finance, Bill worked in a local bank during school as an assistant in the loan department. His job involved talking with people about different types of loans. He would then come up with a recommendation and present it to the loan officer for review and approval of the customer.

After graduation, Bill took a job at the family business. He now helps his father by gathering financial information from the firm's customers. Then he helps determine what the best plan is for the individual's financial needs. In order to increase the number of clients for the firm's services, Bill teaches a finance course to adults through a local organization. The course is designed to educate people about the various methods of investing. During the course, he talks about such things as the stock market, portfolios, retirement plans, and handling college costs.

Bill really enjoys his job and hopes to help his father expand the business and even hire additional employees. He feels that good communication skills are essential in being a good financial planner. According to Bill, you must be able to talk with your customers even about difficult financial matters, and you also must have strong writing skills in order to send out letters outlining financial options.

What It Takes to Be a Financial Planner

This is a profession that requires a diverse set of skills. Financial planners need to be knowledgeable about stocks, bonds, mutual funds, real estate, insurance, taxes, and trusts. They need to be skilled at working with numbers and be able to understand complicated legal and financial documents. In today's world, they must be computer literate, which includes the ability to research financial information on the Internet and create spreadsheets and word-processing documents.

Because planners must be well informed about current economic conditions and trends, a college education is almost a prerequisite in this profession. Majors in business, finance, and economics are helpful, along with with some classes in communications, management, and computers. Plus many financial planners take additional course work or training in insurance, securities, taxes, and real estate. Once financial planners have worked in the field for a few years, one option for advancement is to obtain a master's degree in financial planning through a program such as the College for Financial Planning in Denver. The sixteen graduate-level courses provide practical information useful in expanding a client base or developing a specialization in the dynamic field of financial planning.

Personal qualities are also important in this career. Professional planners need to have initiative and be able to work well with people as well as independently. They also need to be articulate and persuasive and have sales ability in order to build a clientele. And of course, they need to be mature.

Certification

Just as the CPA designation indicates that an accountant has a certain expertise, the Certified Financial Planner (CFP) designation shows that a financial planner is well qualified. This is an extremely important designation as there are not any state licensing requirements in this profession at the present time. Anyone can now call himself or herself a financial planner, and some will not have the skills that this profession demands. There are now more than thirty-one thousand CFPs in the United States.

Requirements for the CFP Designation

CFP candidates must complete a comprehensive course of education in the fundamentals of financial planning, insurance planning, investment planning, income tax planning, retirement planning and employee benefits, and estate planning at an approved university or college.

After completing the approved course of education, candidates are eligible to sit for the certification examination, which is a ten-hour test taken over two days. The certification examination is designed to assess the planner's ability to apply financial planning education to financial planning situations in an integrated format, thereby protecting the public by assuring that they are at the appropriate level of competency required for practice.

To actually use the CFP designation in public practice, the licensee must also have a bachelor's degree plus three years experience in the financial services sector, or five years full-time experience in the financial planning field without a bachelor's degree. CFP licensees must complete a minimum of thirty hours continuing education every two years and sign and adhere to a code of ethics that demands full disclosure, integrity, competence, objectivity, fairness, confidentiality, professionalism, and diligence in the performance of their duties.

Additional Certification

Since states have bonding and licensing requirements for people who buy and sell stocks, bonds, and securities, individuals working in these areas will have to get the appropriate licensing. In addition, many financial planners are CPAs and a few are Chartered Financial Analysts (CFAs).

Qualifications

If you look at the want ads in a newspaper or visit one of the large job boards on the Internet, you will quickly see that employers have set high standards for the type of employees they are seeking as financial planners for their firms. Note the skills, certification, and education that employers were looking for in the following advertisements for experienced financial planners.

CERTIFIED FINANCIAL PLANNER LICENSEE   Ten-year-old fee-first planning firm needs an experienced CFP. Enjoy the California beaches and help build your practice. Prefer three to five years' experience. Strong computer skills a must.

Manager of Client Services   The manager of client Services will provide financial planning, client service, and administrative support to the principal of a rapidly growing financial advisory firm. This position provides an opportunity to learn all aspects of the investment advisory business and contribute significantly to the company's growth. Principal responsibilities include:

- Maintain good communication with current clients through ongoing mailings and phone calls (articles, cards, reports, and other documents)

- Respond to client requests for special reports, distributions

- Schedule and confirm client appointments

- Maintain client and vendor files

- Prepare materials and reports for quarterly client meetings

- Maintain balance sheet on each client and detailed asset tracking

- Use software tools to develop tax plans, retirement plans, and charitable-giving illustrations

- Document the work process and improvement efforts

Qualifications include:

- Initiative and a strong desire to learn

- College degree and/or appropriate experience in financial field

- Strong computer background (i.e. Word, Excel, ACT, Internet, Quicken, etc.)

- Certified Financial Planner (CFP) designation or a willingness to work toward such designation

- Successful completion of the NASD Series 7 test desirable

INTERNAL DIRECTOR OF FINANCIAL PLANNING We are a nationally prominent fee-based financial planning firm, regularly listed among the top planners in the country and achieving the expected publicity that comes with those honors. Our mission is to help our clients (typically corporate executives, business owners, and professionals with healthy incomes and net worths) develop and implement strategies to attain their personal goals. We view ourselves primarily as a financial planning firm, but enjoy a substantial income from fees derived from managing more than $80 million of client investments.

To support our continued growth, we need to hire someone to work internally in our six-person office, doing the actual financial analysis and plan preparation and acting as the day-to-day supervisor of the client portfolios. All would be under my direct supervision. While the maintenance and development of good client relations will be important, no outside client development will be expected of this person, since the number of opportunities that already exist are sufficient to keep us all busy.

The person I am looking for would ideally be an experienced CFP, personable, detail oriented, a good writer, computer savvy, cooperative, creative, self-motivated, loyal, hard working, and knowledgeable regarding income and estate taxes and investments. A good fit with our growing six-person staff in a hard-working, dynamic, positive environment would be important. Salary is negotiable. If you have existing clients, we could talk about how to fit them into our system with appropriate compensation to you.

Four Practicing Financial Planners

The route to becoming a financial planner is different for these four financial planners. Today, all are working alone, which is a popular career route for experienced financial planners. As you read this section, note the certification and educational backgrounds of these planners and the areas in which they specialize as well as their professional affiliations and career advice.

A Background in Banking

Mary Tinter is a certified financial planner who has her own financial planning firm in a small Midwestern city. She left a ten-year banking career to pursue this career. Today, she has twenty clients whom she knows very well. Mary believes that this helps her create the right financial plan for each client's situation. Although Mary has a bachelor's degree in business administration, she has always been interested in taking courses that keep her up-to-date in her profession. After starting her firm, she enrolled in the master's program for financial planning through the College for Financial Planning in Denver and has taken courses in insurance and retirement planning, which are now her specialty areas. In the future, Mary plans to take more courses in such areas as taxes and securities. She also keeps up with the latest in financial planning by being a member of the Association for Financial Planners and the International Association for Financial Planners.

A Background in Banking, Securities, and Financial Consulting

Although Charles O'Kelley works for a financial consulting firm, he has his own office and runs his own business. His educational background consists of a bachelor's degree in political science with a concentration in business and economics courses. In order to keep up with changes in the financial world and guide his clients successfully, he is currently completing the CFP program and plans to enroll in the Chartered Financial Analyst Program (CFA) after he has CFP certification.

His career path has included a variety of financial positions, which has given him expertise in several areas. He began his career in commercial banking, became a financial controller at a company, went to work with Merrill Lynch as an account manager, returned to banking as a bank manager, and then worked as a financial product wholesaler representing firms involved in mutual funds, variable and fixed annuities, and real estate direct participation programs. His final career move was into financial planning working with a group of financial consultants.

On the Job

Charles spends approximately sixty hours each week designing and implementing financial plans for individuals and corporations. In addition to virtually running his own investment company, he is the co-owner of a real estate and mortgage banking business. Charles decided to get involved in real estate because he believes that land and its financing represents the single largest asset of most individuals and businesses and impacts all aspects of financial planning for an individual or corporation.

Pluses and Minuses

Charles finds that his job can sometimes be lonely because he lacks the daily association with other financial planning professionals. He also finds that running your own business can be overwhelming and stressful at times. However, the joy Charles receives when one of his clients fulfills his or her financial objectives and goals makes up for any downsides.

Career Advice

Even though consolidations are occurring in financial services markets and profit margins are shrinking, Charles feels that opportunities for dedicated financial planning professionals who are committed to helping people achieve their financial goals and objective have never been better.

A Background in Corporate Finance

Mike Casper retired after working for twenty-five years as a financial officer for a large manufacturing organization to become a financial consultant. During his last few years with the manufacturing company, he was in charge of keeping all the financial statements for the North American operations. This involved traveling to all the sites of the company, auditing the inventory recorded monthly in financial statements, and talking with upper management about any major increases or decreases in their expenses. In order to help forecast the future financial state of the organization, Mike had to also stay in close contact with the marketing salesperson.

While Mike really enjoyed his job with the company, he was ready to work on his own and help others meet their financial goals. He started his financial consultant business by helping a friend set up a small card store. Now almost five years later, Mike has helped more than fifty companies start up new businesses or expand their businesses. He especially enjoys working with smaller companies. Mike also likes being his own boss and being able to set his work hours.

In order to make his business a success, Mike had to effectively communicate his strong financial skills and business successes to the community. This was probably the most challenging part of starting out as a consultant. After working with a few friends and relatives, the word slowly started to spread about his expertise. Now Mike even advertises in magazines and newspapers to find new clients.

Career Advice

Mike says that you must believe in yourself. When things seem to be moving slowly, he advises you to keep pushing and working hard, as it will eventually pay off.

A Background in Life Insurance and Securities

When Gordon Peay writes his name, he can follow it with the designations CLU (Chartered Life Underwriter), ChFC (Chartered Financial Consultant), and CFP (Certified Financial Planner), indicating the high level of expertise he brings to his career as a financial planner. Not only are his credentials impressive, he has contributed to the development of his profession by serving as the president and then the chair of the board of the Los Angeles Society of the Institute of Certified Financial Planners. The mission of this organization is to promote a higher level of consumer awareness and confidence and to provide timely, relevant financial planning information to consumers. The organization holds symposiums on a wide variety of financial planning and investment topics, hosts events to encourage and enhance relationships with other professionals such as CPAs and attorneys, maintains a speakers bureau and a Web site (http://www.LAICFP.org), and produces a monthly newsletter.

Gordon owns his own financial planning firm, The Capital Advantage. He gained the knowledge that he uses every day initially by working first as a life insurance agent and then as a securities sales representative. He also believes that much of what he has learned of the entire investment spectrum can be attributed to frequent lunches with a good friend who is a certified financial analyst and an investment guru. Networking is valuable in finance.

Owning his own business means long ten- and twelve-hour days for Gordon plus some work on weekends. With each new client, he goes through the following steps:

1. helps the client establish and define financial goals

2. drafts balance sheet showing client's present financial status

3. develops one or two strategies to help the client reach his or her financial goals, which often includes recommendations on saving, investment allocation, insurance, and taxes

4. determines most advantageous plan with client

5. handles the necessary tasks (investments, wills, trusts, insurance) to implement the plan

6. keeps records of discussions and all financial transactions

7. meets annually or more frequently with client to review financial status

Career Advice

Everyone is responsible for his or her own destiny. As investment alternatives and strategies become more complex, many people will look to financial planners for help in achieving their goals.

Professional Organizations

There are organizations for financial planners that offer them ways to learn how to grow their businesses, increase their professional knowledge, and build contacts with other allied professionals. These organizations offer newsletters, magazines, seminars, professional development courses, and comprehensive insurance benefits for members. To gain membership in these organizations, it is essential to meet certain professional qualifications. Two organizations that will keep you abreast of what is happening in this profession are the Institute of Certified Financial Planners (ICFP) and the International Association for Financial Planning (IAFP).

Climbing the Career Ladder

The principal form of advancement for financial planners is by expanding the areas of their expertise and thus increasing the range of financial services or products they handle. Beginning financial planners will usually start with individual accounts and work toward handling very large institutional accounts. In some companies, the ability to generate high commissions can lead to positions as branch office managers and supervisors. A few select financial planners will advance to top management positions. Many will elect to start their own businesses.

Since financial planners combine formal education with experience in one or more areas of finance—such as asset management, lending, credit operations, securities investments, or insurance risk and loss control—financial planners can leave the profession to become budget officers, credit analysts, loan officers, insurance consultants, portfolio managers, pension consultants, real estate advisors, securities analysts, and underwriters.

Employment Trends and Salaries

How much you will be able to earn as a financial planner depends to a great degree on the type of firm you work for. Each company has its own pay structure. There are three common salary structures:

- Base—earn a set salary for a specified period of time

- Base + commissions—receive a base salary, but if you sell a product or receive a fee, anything over the amount of your base is split with the company

- Commissions only—do not receive any compensation unless you sell a product or receive a fee

An average financial planner just starting out can expect to earn in the range of $25,000 to $33,000. This will quickly jump with experience. Depending on the ambition of the financial planner, annual compensation can range from $50,000 to $100,000 after only five years. Some financial institutions and companies offer benefits that include paid holidays and vacations, health and life insurance, and pension plans.

Many financial managers in private industry receive additional compensation in the form of bonuses, which many also vary substantially by the size of the firm. If you go into business for yourself, you can usually expect lower income your first few years until you have built up a strong client base. Once you have many good clients and a solid reputation, your income limits are endless.

More Career Information

By contacting the following organizations, you should be able to get more information on a career in financial planning:

Financial Management Association International
College of Business Administration
University of South Florida
Tampa, FL 33620-5500

Institute of Certified Financial Planners
7600 East Eastman Ave., Suite 301
Denver, CO 80231-4397

International Association for Financial Planning
Two Concourse Pkwy., Suite 800
Atlanta, GA 30328

CHAPTER SEVEN

Working at a Bank

The Diverse Jobs of Bank Employees

S ince its inception by the Babylonians more than four thousand years ago, banking has been designed to meet people's needs to borrow and hold money. The Romans extended the services the first banks provided to include transferring accounts, making loans, and letting people write checks to withdraw funds. The word *bank* did not emerge until the Middle Ages, when it was used to describe the activities of Italian money changers who sat behind benches (*bancos*). As trade routes sprang up, banking systems began evolving in other countries. English traders stored their precious metals in the goldsmith's vaults and in return the goldsmith gave them receipts for the gold and silver which were more convenient to carry around. The goldsmiths began lending out the stored precious metals and gave interest to the people who had stored the metals in their vaults.

Banking in America

The early American colonists didn't use banks because bartering handled their needs. The first banks to be set up in this country were land banks to provide loans to farmers, followed by banks to provide cash for commerce. Unfortunately, the king of England closed all the colonial banks, and there wasn't a true American bank until the Bank of North America in Philadelphia was chartered by the Congressional Congress. By the time of the Civil

War, banks really had only two main functions, making loans and accepting deposits, which they are still doing today. In fact, most banking was done on a cash basis until checking accounts became popular in the late 1870s. Then banks began to offer other services like personal and short term loans.

Today, banks provide a wide range of services to both businesses and individuals with their drive-through windows, automatic teller machines (ATMs), credit cards, travelers' checks, portfolio management, special savings accounts, financing, on-line banking, direct deposits, bill paying, and even banking centers in grocery stores. Banking has become a very competitive business in which banks compete for customers by the services they offer, which includes friendly, pleasant, and efficient help. Furthermore, new innovations are constantly springing up to capture more customers.

A Look at Where the Jobs Are

If you are a money mover, then a job at a bank could be perfect for you because money is the business of banks. You could work in a community bank that concentrates on serving local residents and businesses, a larger bank that serves both individuals and businesses, or a credit union or savings and loan association that performs many of the same functions as banks. There are both small and large savings and loan associations, which primarily use the funds deposited in them for residential loans. Credit unions, which also vary in size, are made up of members who use their savings to make low-cost loans to each other.

Working Conditions

Bankers once only worked in banks. Today, you can find them outside traditional bank settings in places like shopping malls and grocery stores. Bankers generally work during the day, Monday through Friday; however, some evening and weekend work may be required. As long as banks are open, there will be bankers on duty, and the trend is for banks to stay open longer hours and on Saturdays.

Tellers

To be a successful teller, you need to be a high school graduate and have certain skills. As you might expect, you need to be a detail-oriented person. You also should have good math skills, and banks prefer you to have had classes in accounting, bookkeeping, economics, computers, and public speaking. Because you will be dealing with the public, it is essential that you be a courteous, attentive, and patient individual. And of course, you need to feel comfortable handling large amounts of cash. In some areas, an ability to speak a second language is definitely a plus.

Starting as a Teller

Eight years ago, Betty Pachciarz became a teller. She attended a two-week training class; however, today new tellers at her bank learn their job responsibilities through a ten-day computer program that they complete at their own pace. In addition to handling her job as a full-service teller, Betty now provides on-the-job training to new tellers after they have completed the computer program. Her regular duties include cashing checks, taking deposits, issuing cashier checks and money orders, and answering customers' questions about their accounts. She also accepts payment for customers' utility bills, keeps records, and completes the necessary paperwork for customer loans. In addition, she processes certificates of deposit and money market accounts and sells travelers' checks.

Betty, like all tellers, must be very precise in her work. Before she can cash a check, she must verify the date, bank names, and identity of the person to receive payment; see that the document is legal tender; that written and numerical amounts agree; and that the account has sufficient funds to cover the check. Only then does Betty carefully count out the cash to avoid errors. Sometimes a customer withdraws money in the form of a cashier's check, which she prepares and verifies. When accepting a deposit, she always checks the accuracy of the deposit slip before processing the transaction. In some banks, they still type or write out deposit receipts and passbook entries by hand, but this is uncommon. In most banks, like Betty's, tellers use computer terminals to record deposits and withdrawals. Some banks use very sophisticated computer systems that give tellers quick access to detailed information on customer accounts. Tellers may use this information to tailor their services to fit the customer's needs or recommend an appropriate bank product or service.

On the Job with a Teller

Betty's duties start before the bank opens and end after the bank closes if she is working a full day. Many of the tellers work part-time at her bank. She begins her day by receiving and counting an amount of working cash for her drawer; this amount is verified by a supervisor, usually the head teller. She will use this cash for payments during the day and is responsible for its safe and accurate handling. At the end of her banking day, Betty counts the cash she has on hand, lists the currency-received tickets on a balance sheet, and balances the day's accounts. She also sorts checks and deposit slips.

Betty likes working with the bank's customers even though it can be difficult to deal with some of them. She finds that she no longer just handles people's immediate needs but now must also be an avid salesperson, promoting additional bank products and services because of all the competition for customers between banks. Because banks are now offering more and increasingly complex financial services, most bank tellers, like Betty, are now being trained to act as customer service representatives in addition to their other duties.

Career Path

Advancement opportunities are good for well-trained, motivated tellers. They can advance to positions as head teller, customer service representative, or new accounts clerk. At Betty's bank there are three levels of tellers. You can move up the ladder from a full-service teller to a vault teller, which will require you to keep track of all the money that comes in and out of the branch. A step higher is the new accounts clerk. In this job, you will handle opening new accounts, work with certificates of deposits (CDs) and individual retirement accounts (IRAs), and set up trusts and loan installments.

Outstanding tellers who have had some college or specialized training offered by the banking industry may be promoted to a managerial position. Banks encourage this upward mobility by providing access to education and other sources of additional training. Through the American Institute of Banking, an educational affiliate of the American Bankers Association, or the Institute of Financial Education, tellers can participate in numerous study groups and take correspondence courses. In addition, many banks refund college tuition fees to their employees upon successful completion of courses.

Employment Opportunities for Tellers

Bank tellers hold more than half a million jobs today; however, more than one-fourth of them work part-time. If you are seriously considering a career as a teller, opportunities for employment should be good if you have the necessary qualifications, even though employment in this field is expected to decline for a variety of reasons. There are fewer banks as more banks consolidate and many branches are closed. Furthermore, new technology in this area is also decreasing the demand for tellers. Some banks have introduced branches that consist entirely of ATMs and kiosks, further reducing the need for tellers. There are also banks which provide many services, once done by tellers, by computer or telephone. Banks are also opening branches inside supermarkets and department stores that have ATMs and more highly trained customer service representatives who can perform the standard duties of tellers and also open new accounts and arrange for customers to receive other services or products sold by the bank.

Many job openings will arise from the need to replace tellers who transfer to other occupations or stop working. Turnover is high in occupations like teller because the pay is low and little formal education is required. Banks, on the other hand, are having problems finding tellers because the duties of these workers have become more complex.

Earnings for Tellers

The starting salary for bank tellers is approximately $7.00 an hour. Many banks, however, are now offering incentives that allow tellers to earn supplemental rewards for inducing customers to use other financial products and services offered by the bank. In general, tellers who have a greater range of responsibilities are receiving the higher salaries. Experience, length of service, and especially the location and size of the bank also are important in determining earnings. Part-time tellers do not always have benefits but may receive higher hourly earnings in place of the benefits.

Branch Services Representatives

Working at a Neighborhood Bank

Isidra Collins is a branch services representative at a small neighborhood bank. In her bank, this job carries the same responsibilities that assistant managers typically have. Isidra handles a little bit of everything, as she must be able to run the branch in the absence of the branch manager. She deals with problems in customer services, opens new accounts, balances the bank funds, oversees the tellers in the absence of the manager, and must run a teller's window when her branch is short of help. Isidra works from 8:30 A.M. to 5:30 P.M. Monday through Friday. When she works on Saturday, she gets a day off during the week. She also has an hour break for lunch.

Career Path

Isidra began her career in banking as a part-time teller in a neighborhood branch of a large Ohio bank. She got the job because she passed the bank's math test and had demonstrated her ability to handle money through a previous job as a grocery store cashier. When her husband was transferred to another state, she took a job as a drive-through window teller at a local bank. Within a few months, another position opened up and she was able to start moving up the teller ladder toward her present position. Isidra attributes the promotion to her present job to taking classes in customer services and learning how to open new accounts.

Job Skills

In her present position as branch services representative, Isidra needs to have good communication skills and knowledge of all the products available at the bank. She also has to have the know-how to make the branch run efficiently. In addition, she must have the maturity and tact to deal with difficult customers. While on the job, Isidra must be able to move quickly from one task to another. She frequently has to stop what she is doing and attend to the needs of a customer.

With so many things to do, Isidra must have solid organizational skills to prioritize her tasks. Every day on the job, she faces the challenge of keeping customers happy and earning their loyalty to this branch bank. Although most banks are bursting with technological equipment, at her small branch it is sufficient to know how to use an adding machine.

Bank Management

Bank officers carry out their board of directors' policies on a daily basis and make their decisions in accordance with these policies and federal and state laws and regulations. The larger a bank is, the larger its management team will be and the more services it will offer, from dealing with foreign currency to payroll deposits. The officers that you will find in all but the smallest banks include:

- Loan officers, who evaluate the credit and collateral of people and businesses applying for loans

- Trust officers, who administer estates and trusts, manage property, invest funds for clients, and provide financial counseling

- Operations officers, who plan and coordinate procedures and systems

- Cashiers, who are responsible for all bank property

- Branch managers, who have responsibility for bank operations

Other bank officers in large banks handle auditing, personnel administration, public relations, employee benefits, credit, branch administration, marketing, international banking, Internet and electronic banking, and research. In the giant banks that have been formed in recent mergers, you will not just find one officer in a department, but hundreds.

Do you think that you have the necessary skills to become a bank officer? Take this quiz to find out.

- Are you willing to earn an M.B.A. degree?

- Do you have analytical skills?

- Do you have detailed knowledge of the banking industry?

- Are you willing to gain certification in specialized fields to exhibit your competency?

- Do you have detailed information about the industries allied to banking?

- Are you willing to keep abreast of new bank products and technology?

- Do you know the latest financial analysis methods?

- Do you possess solid management techniques?

If you feel that you possess most of these skills, then a career as a bank officer may be the right goal for you.

A Young Banker Starting His Management Career

Matt Zigler has been out of school for less than a year, and he has already moved up the career ladder to become an assistant manager at a branch of a large bank. He began his banking career as a retail associate after graduating from college with a bachelor's degree in economics and music. A retail associate is a manager in training. Matt began by training as a teller and was then given the opportunity to work in all the different departments of the bank, including mortgage, operations, private banking, collections, and securities. He also had the opportunity to go out to several branches and work one-on-one with the managers and tellers and learn their duties and how to process transactions. The training period gave Matt an overview of how each bank department runs. Furthermore, he had the opportunity to make contacts in each department. As assistant manager, Matt's responsibilities now include:

- operating the branch

- ordering cash

- receiving shipments of cash

- making sure the tellers balance daily

- balancing the vault daily

- changing the security videos every week

- auditing the whole banking center

- taking care of collections items

- reporting all outages (when tellers' accounts don't balance)

- scheduling three tellers

- overseeing the tellers

- opening all new accounts

- checking savings, trusts, and IRA accounts

- processing loans

- taking care of problems of angry customers

- meeting goals, which includes opening a certain number of new accounts

Reflections on His Career

Even though his job requires fifty- to sixty-hour work weeks, Matt is very pleased that he is already in a management position. In the future, he would like to become a branch manager. A lot of people working for banks today are young, like Matt. He believes that you have an opportunity to move up faster in a small bank and likes knowing everyone in the bank. And Matt has definitely discovered that his job is not monotonous. Something new and different is always happening. He has found the amount of information he is expected to know to be mind-boggling. Matt only had five weeks of training, yet his customers expect him to know everything about banking, and he doesn't. He feels challenged by this steep learning curve and at times overwhelmed by it. The one avenue of banking that surprised Matt was the heavy emphasis on sales. He is constantly required to push loans, get new accounts, and promote products and services that the customers do not currently have. One problem area that bothers Matt is the constant turnover of tellers. He just gets a teller trained to the level where he or she can work well independently and then the teller leaves so he has to start all over again training a new teller.

Career Advice

If you are considering becoming a branch manager, Matt recommends taking public speaking and writing courses because communication is so important in this career. Also, he believes that you should be flexible and have good people skills and a solid code of ethics.

A Banking Center Manager and Loan Officer

Matt Broughton works in a grocery store; however, he is not stocking the shelves or ringing up your purchases, instead he is walking up and down the aisles trying to get new customers into his bankmart (a bank housed inside a grocery store). He is one of two managers who keep this bank open seven days a week starting as early as 9:00 A.M. on Saturdays and not closing until 8:00 P.M. during the week. One of the managers must always be at the bank so if one is on vacation, the other may work a ten-hour day. Usually, the two managers' schedules overlap between 2:00 P.M. and 4:00 P.M. so they have a time to talk. Both managers report to a regional officer who is in charge of all eleven bankmarts in grocery stores in Indiana.

As manager, Matt is in charge of the profitability of his banking center, which means he must meet certain goals for bringing in new customers. He also wears two hats when he acts as loan officer. Not only does he investigate loan applicants, he also approves them for loans. Matt has to really know the loan applicants because if they fail to repay, the loan is charged against his profits. Matt always makes an extremely careful investigation of applicants. He determines if they live close to the bank, what their lifestyle is, how long they have lived in their homes, and whether they have bad credit ratings and, if so, why.

Career Path

Matt started in banking immediately after graduating from college, and this is his first job illustrating that there are excellent opportunities in banking for young people. When he was halfway through college, he decided that he wanted a career in finance and secured three internships in this area. The first was at a large bank where he was able to spend a few days in each area, which really gave him a good feel for banking. Next, he worked with an independent financial broker. His last internship was with a large insurance company where he worked an entire summer. Matt was hired individually by different agents, and his job was to do what they wanted, whether it was to send out mailers, work on a portfolio, fold letters, or talk to a customer. Although he felt that for the most part he was really doing grunt work, the internship exposed him to the selling of financial products.

Matt plans to return to school in three or four years to get his M.B.A. His bank will reimburse him for the cost; however, he will have to work a few additional years at the bank after receiving this degree.

The salary range for a branch manager is from $38,000 to $50,000 at banks with large assets. It will be as much as 15 percent less at small banks.

Career Advice

Matt feels that you need to have good time management and organizational skills to be a bank manager. He also says that you shouldn't expect to use the academic skills you learned in economic theory class when you are just starting out.

Chief Executive Officer at a Small Bank

While growing up on a farm, Tom McCartan really never thought about a career in banking. His father, however, taught him the importance of working hard and being good at what you do. This gave Tom the drive to be the best he could be. After a stint in the army, he graduated from college with a degree in finance and accounting. Tom then talked to the president of a small agricultural bank back in his hometown and got a job as an officer trainee. He attributes most of what he knows about banking to the knowledge he gained from watching upper management and the training he received at the bank. Also, since Tom grew up on a farm, he did have the advantage of understanding the farming business. This is extremely important since more than 70 percent of the business at this bank is with agriculture.

After Tom had worked at the bank only a few years, the president who had hired him left. This put the bank into a bind. Tom and a former bank employee decided to buy the bank. He became vice president and some years later chief executive officer (CEO).

On the Job as CEO

As the owner of the bank, Tom says that every day is interesting and new. He is never sure what to expect. Tom starts his workday with a staff meeting, which allows him to see the updates on any loans or investments. His next step is to go through the mail and take care of any important issues that may have come up. Depending on the customers' needs that day, Tom may spend some time talking with them explaining how many of the bank's services could help their individual situations. Other important tasks that Tom is responsible for include trying to get new loan applications, talking to borrowers, closing bad loans, reviewing credit files, getting new cash flows for loans, taking care of trustee assets, and updating all bank files.

Tom really likes the interaction that he has with his customers. Since the bank is a smaller bank that closely fits the needs of the farming industry, he has the opportunity to really get to know and work with his customers. During slower times of the year, Tom goes out of the bank with a few of his staff members to interact with customers. In the summer, it is not unusual to see him up on a tractor talking with them. In this way, he really learns a lot about the people he deals with and their jobs. Another technique that Tom has used to keep everyone at the bank in touch with customers and potential customers is establishing clubs and organizations that put on seminars. These seminars provide information regarding long-term care insurance and other important issues that his customers may need. The bank also puts on a Pork Fest every year for the town.

Tom enjoys being able to take part in all aspects of the banking industry. He points out that in large banks an employee will become proficient in one area, while in a small bank, everyone gets the opportunity to perform all the tasks. Not only does this keep them up-to-date on what is going on, it also gives them a wide skill base.

Career Advice

Once you have a good job, Tom urges you to continue to set goals. He feels that it is important to have something to strive for.

Vice President of Operations

John Dee is the vice president of operations at the thirty-fifth-largest bank in America. He is in charge of retail banking, banking offices, consumer lending, and anything to do with consumers or small businesses. He feels like he is on the job twenty-four hours a day and can never totally separate home and work. When he is away from the office at church or an event, he is always aware of potential opportunities to promote the bank. On the job, technology plays a very significant role as a tool that can be used in cost management and cost reduction. It also lets his bank bring new products to the market quickly, which is the key to customer service. Today's bank customers want information, and they want it quickly. John believes that technology is the answer in providing customer service. With the current strong economy, one of the greatest challenges in John's job is being able to attract and keep good employees. While in the past it was sufficient for job candidates to have good people skills, now they need sales and promotional skills to be effective in bank management jobs.

Skills and Experiences

Not only does John have an M.B.A. in finance, he also has a doctorate in finance. While it is not necessary to have a doctorate, the knowledge that he gained in earning this degree has been very helpful in the business arena. John began his climb to the top by working in the steel mills. Then he became a professor at a university and the chief economist for a bank. His resume also includes owning an investment advisory company, managing mutual funds, and serving as the president of a savings and loan association. If you wish to hold a high-level management position as John does, it is essential to build an impressive resume.

Pluses and Minuses

John likes that his company does not just tell the officers what to do but also provides the support to tell them how to do it with ongoing classes taught throughout the region. He is delighted to be working in central Indiana, which has a solid economy. Furthermore, he enjoys the special partnership he has with the headquarters of the bank. John believes that he gets a lot of support and truly enjoys working with the wonderful people at his bank. For him, it is a real pleasure to come to work each day. On the negative side, John dislikes the overload of information—so much E-mail and so many phone calls and letters. Sometime he finds himself overwhelmed trying to keep up with the flow of information.

Career Advice

John feels that the only constant is change and that future bank managers must be flexible and adapt to change. He advises you to give 110 percent in your work because it will pay off. John also wants you to have a great attitude, the ability to focus and prioritize, good people skills, and the ability to motivate and lead people.

Bank Loan Officers

Being a loan officer is an important position at a bank, for it is loans that are the major source of income for banks. Loan officers typically specialize in one of three fields: commercial, consumer, or mortgage loans. If you want to borrow money to buy a car, you would deal with a consumer loan officer. In order to purchase a home, it would be a mortgage loan officer. Businesses work with commercial loan officers.

Loan officers have the responsibility of meeting with customers and gathering basic information about the loan request. Frequently, they will have to help the prospective borrower fill out the loan forms. Once the forms are complete, the loan officer begins to process them. After checking the application for completeness and accuracy, the loan officer requests a credit check from one or more major credit-reporting agencies. All of this information is put into the loan file and compared to the requirements that the bank has established for granting loans. At this point, the loan officer, in consultation with his or her manager, decides whether or not to grant the loan.

Loan officers usually carry heavy caseloads and sometimes cannot accept new clients until they complete current cases. They are especially busy when interest rates are low, resulting in a surge in loan applications. As a loan officer, you would usually work in an office; however, mortgage loan officers frequently move from bank to bank and may even visit clients in their homes. Commercial loan officers at large banks will travel to prepare complex loan agreements.

Job Qualifications for Loan Officers

You will almost always need to be a college graduate in order to become a loan officer; however, some tellers and customer service representatives do advance to this position. Because you will be dealing with the public, you should be able to establish good relationships with people. It's also important to be a gregarious person who enjoys contact with people, for you will be attending community events as a representative of your bank. If you want to become a mortgage loan officer, sales training and experience are important. It is also important for all loan officers to be familiar with computers and their applications in banking. Your background for this position needs to include mathematical skills and good oral and written communications skills.

Employment Opportunities

There are more than two hundred thousand loan officers in the United States. They don't just work at banks but also at savings and loans associations and credit unions. Others are employed by nonbank financial institutions, such as mortgage brokerage firms and personal credit firms. Jobs as loan officers are usually found in urban areas where large banks and other financial institutions are concentrated.

Capable loan officers may advance to larger branches of the firm or to a managerial position, while less capable loan officers and those having inadequate academic preparation may be assigned to smaller branches and find promotion difficult. Advancement from a loan officer position usually includes becoming a supervisor over other loan officers and clerical staff. Your chances of advancement are enhanced if you become a Certified Lender in Business Banking. This certification is earned through courses offered by the American Institute of Banking.

The future appears bright for loan officers as employment is expected to grow faster than for most other occupations. As the population and economy grow, applications for commercial, consumer, and mortgage loans will increase, spurring demand for loan officers. Growth in the variety and complexity of loans and the importance of loan officers to the success of banks and other lending institutions also should assure rapid employment growth. Although increased demand will generate many new jobs, most openings will result from the need to replace workers who leave the occupation or retire.

Earnings

The form of compensation for loan officers varies, depending on the lending institution. Some banks offer salary plus commission as an incentive to increase the number of loans processed, while others pay only salaries.

According to a salary survey conducted by Robert Half International, a staffing services firm specializing in accounting and finance, residential real estate mortgage loan officers earn between $37,000 and $47,000; commercial real estate mortgage loan officers earn between $54,000 and $74,000; and consumer loan officers earn between $35,000 and $49,000. These salaries are for banks with assets of more than $1 billion. Expect to earn as much as 15 percent less if you work for a bank with assets of $100 million or less.

A Look at the Future

Banks have changed greatly in the 1990s. Mergers and acquisitions have led to the establishment of giant banking firms. This has resulted in the closing of many branch banks when services were duplicated in a community, as well as staff reduction at the headquarters of the consolidated banks. At the same time, a number of small community banks have emerged that stress customer service. Another revolution that has affected the banking industry is the rush to offer more and more services, especially on-line banking. Banking is now a very competitive industry. Career opportunities are especially good for those who have computer skills that can put banks on-line and personalities that will shine in the marketing and sales of new bank products.

CHAPTER EIGHT

Raising Money for Businesses

The Jobs of Venture Capitalists and Investment Bankers

Y ou have a bright idea about building a revolutionary new bicycle frame that is just one piece. You show it to several bicycle manufacturers, and they think that you have a hot product. The problem: you simply don't have the money to start making frames in any quantity. Here's another scenario. You have started a restaurant that features a brand new concept—food cooked under rocks. People are flocking to your restaurant to get this unusual fare. You want to launch similar restaurants in several other locations. The problem: you don't have the money to expand into new areas. Traditional banks are rarely enthusiastic about loaning money for fledgling businesses, but venture capitalists are often willing to provide start-ups or promising new companies with money in exchange for a share of the company.

Perhaps, instead of having a new company, you own a huge, well-established food company that needs millions of dollars to buy a very large bakery that will let you expand the line of products that your company carries. Or your company may need to build a warehouse to serve as a modern distribution center for your food products. Again, you need very large sums of money. In either case, you may go to an investment bank that will help you establish a strategy for getting the money you need and serve as an intermediary in getting the money for you.

It is the venture capitalists and investment bankers who help businesses raise the money they need. These are not large professions, but they are challenging, dynamic professions that require bright people with abundant energy to handle the fast pace of careers in this area. They are great jobs for financial mavens who want to discover and finance the next Microsoft.

A Closer Look at Venture Capitalism

Very wealthy individuals, corporations, pension funds, and college endowments are just some of the investors in venture capital firms. They provide this money knowing that there is a high risk that a new business venture will not succeed. What causes them to make these risky investments is knowing the high return that will be earned if a business succeeds. Venture capitalism is a high-risk, high-rewards business.

These firms don't just invest in companies when they are starting up, they invest in companies when they have developed a product; have started to sell a product, but have little income; are rapidly expanding; and are getting ready to sell shares to the public. The way that venture capital firms make money is by selling their shares in a company after it has gone public for more money than they invested in the company.

Having a promising idea or a solid young business is no guarantee that a company or individual will receive any of the billions of dollars invested by venture capital firms each year. To get the money they need to finance their ideas, the companies must demonstrate to the venture capitalists that they have an outstanding product and a solid business plan. Besides providing money, venture capitalists usually sit on the board of directors of the companies they invest in, providing them with valuable business expertise in addition to financial backing.

Where the Jobs Are

The number-one location of venture capital firms is in Northern California in Silicon Valley and San Francisco. This is where these firms fueled a revolution in technology. They helped such industry giants as Apple Computer, Silicon Graphics, Intel, Netscape, and Genentech get started

If you don't want to work on the West Coast, Boston is the spot to be on the East Coast, closely followed by New York. You will also find a sizable number of venture capital firms in Los Angeles, Philadelphia, and Chicago. Include in your job search areas like Minnesota, Texas, Utah, Washington, and Colorado, where there is high entrepreneurial growth.

Venture capital firms are not the only groups investing money in companies for a share of the company. You could find a job in venture capitalism at affiliates of investment banks, insurance companies, pension funds, universities, and venture divisions of corporations and banks. Because the venture capital field is very small, there are not a great number of jobs.

The Background You Need

In order to get a job in venture capitalism, you will have to demonstrate that you are a bright, articulate person. Furthermore, you will have to show that you have the potential to recognize which start-up firms will be successful and to develop skills so that you can serve as an advisor to help young businesses succeed. If you are to climb the career ladder, you will almost certainly need an M.B.A. degree. It will also be helpful if you have experience in an industry.

The entry-level job in venture capitalism is typically as an analyst, the next step is associate, and then you may become a junior partner. When venture capitalists reach the top rungs of their firms, many leave to start their own firms.

Study the following ads for venture capitalist positions to learn more about what your responsibilities would be and what skills these companies are seeking.

ANALYST   Our firm has been helping early-stage health care companies on the road to success since the 1980s. We focus on medical devices, health care services, and health care information technology, investing from $1 million to $10 million in funding in different stages of financing. The primary responsibilities of the analyst will be to analyze business plans, perform industry and competitive analysis, and work with portfolio companies across functional areas. Analyst candidates should be pre-M.B.A. and have two to three years of management consulting, investment banking, or relevant health care experience. You need to have the ability to work effectively in a fast-paced, rapidly changing environment with minimal supervision. We are seeking an analyst with exceptional communication, analytical, and problem-solving skills.

ASSOCIATE   The subsidiary of a major bank holding company seeks associates to join its venture capital group. The company expects to invest $500 million in the next few years.

Associates will be responsible for analyzing business plans and transactions. Activities will include creating detailed financial models, analysis of comparable companies and transactions, participation in due diligence, and meeting with management, customers, suppliers, and industry experts.

Qualified candidates will have a high level of academic achievement, and a strong work ethic is required. Superior writing skills and familiarity with accounting terminology and database programs are preferred. The ideal candidate should have at least three years' experience in investment banking, merchant banking, consulting, or venture capital.

Investment Banks Are Go-Betweens

Investment banks act as liaisons between large companies that need money and investors that have money. They help the companies get money quickly and efficiently. Investment banks purchase securities such as stocks and bonds from companies and then resell these securities in smaller quantities to investors. Many of these banks also have mergers and acquisitions departments that act as brokers in the buying and selling of companies or parts of companies. They package the company and suggest a sale price if they represent the seller and analyze a company and determine if it is being sold at a fair price if they represent the buyer. If you elect to work at an investment bank, you will be working with millions of dollars every day. This is probably the dream job for all true financial mavens, for no other position will give you such fast exposure to the world of business and finance.

New York Is the Place

Although you could work in an investment bank in Milwaukee, Los Angeles, or Boston, the largest and most prestigious investment banks are headquartered in New York City, and most large investment banks will also have an office there.

A Look at the Career Path for Investment Bankers

Investment banks have a very organized path for advancing up the career ladder. Typically, you begin as an analyst. You will need to be a college graduate with an excellent grade point average and impressive work record and/or extracurricular activities. Investment banks pay well, with analysts at major firms in New York City starting as high as $35,000 to $40,000 annually, plus a substantial bonus after working a year. The analyst position is typically for two or three years. Then most analysts go to business school to get their M.B.A. degrees. The next rung up the ladder is associate. Most associates are hired after they have completed their M.B.A. degrees; however, a few become associates after working as analysts. Starting associates can expect to earn as much as $80,000 a year and will also earn excellent bonuses. After working as an associate for at least three years, the next career step is vice president. Some vice presidents go on to managing director positions; others often elect to take other jobs in the business world.

Working as an Analyst at a Major Investment Bank

With qualifications that included membership in Phi Beta Kappa and leadership roles in college extracurricular activities, Maude Clinton was able to land a position as an analyst at a prestigious investment bank. After just a month of training, she jumped enthusiastically into her job in corporate finance. This department manages securities' offerings for large corporations who want to sell stock or bonds to investors to get more capital for some reason, such as building a new plant. When companies seek financing they go to several investment companies and invite one or more to compete for the job of raising the money they need.

Maude's primary job was working on the preparation of pitch books that outlined how and where the investment bank would get money for a company and why it should be chosen for the deal. These books were used at meetings that senior members of her team had with the companies seeking money. At first, Maude's job was very simple; she checked that all the details in the pitch book were correct. This included such simple tasks as making sure that all the tabs and pages were in place. Although many of the tasks were mindless, she was learning a great deal about finance as she found out why different items were placed in the book.

After a year, she began to get more responsibility. She began to write the first draft of a pitch book. Also, Maude had learned so much about raising money that she was able to make contributions when her team met to discuss a client company.

A Fast-Paced Job

Maude worked from early in the morning until late at night on this job. Her days were packed with activity as she was always working on more than one pitch book at a time. Sometimes she even had to work all night to help get a pitch book completed. And it was very common for her to work on weekends, too. Analysts at investment banks often work eighty-hour weeks.

The Team Approach

At investment banks, people typically work in teams comprised of a vice president, associate, and one or more analysts. Being an associate in corporate finance is basically a four-year apprenticeship in learning how to run a deal. By the time you are a senior associate, you should almost be running deals, which is the ultimate responsibility of the vice president.

A Look at Opportunities

When the economy is robust as it is today, there is a demand for entry-level people in both venture capital and investment bank firms. Innovations in communications and other information technology are fueling the growth of new companies and the expansion of existing companies. Analysts are needed to evaluate businesses and business opportunities for both venture capital firms and investment banks.

CHAPTER NINE

Working in Business Finance

The Jobs of Treasurers, Controllers, and Other Money Movers

P ractically every business and organization has to have one or more individuals involved in handling its financial activities. Manufacturers, stores, hospitals, insurance companies, schools, foundations, charitable organizations, airlines, publishers, hotels, and restaurants—all have a great variety of jobs for money movers. Treasurers, controllers, credit managers, and cash managers are needed to prepare the financial reports required by larger businesses to conduct their operations and to ensure that tax and regulatory requirements have been met. Money movers are also needed to oversee the flow of cash and financial instruments, monitor the extension of credit, assess the risk of transactions, raise capital, analyze investments, develop information to assess the present and future financial status of companies, and communicate with stockholders and other investors. And of course, there is a need for people to handle payroll, pay bills, and keep the books.

Financial mavens can also find jobs at nonprofit organizations overseeing such activities as fund raising, record keeping, financial reporting, investing, and disbursements. In this chapter, we will concentrate on describing jobs in the business arena; many of the same jobs exist in organizations from the Girl Scouts to the Ford Foundation to universities.

Financial Jobs at Very Small Businesses

The store on the corner, the neighborhood restaurant or cleaners, the auto repair shop, and self-employed architects are small businesses in which the owner is doing most of the financial work. An outside bookkeeper may be employed to handle the records and possibly the taxes. When the number of employees increases beyond three or four, an outside payroll service is frequently used to do the required forms, filings, and reports.

As a small business grows, the first person to be hired to do financial and other work is an office manager who assumes the bookkeeping function and may also do the payroll. The owner, however, will keep his or her hand on the financial pulse of the business by signing all the checks, which lets the owner see where the money is being spent.

The first true financial professional to join the staff of a small business is a controller or chief accountant. Unlike an office manager who has other responsibilities, this person will work full-time on financial matters such as keeping the books, paying bills, collecting from customers, doing the billing, and possibly handling the payroll. If the business is big enough, an accounting clerk will be hired to help with the postings and run reports.

Controller at a Small Travel Firm

As controller, Jim Leung does the financial work at a small, but rapidly growing travel firm. He is responsible for:

- managing all financial reporting and accounting systems

- overseeing daily cash management of company operations

- analyzing monthly corporate statements, cash flows, and balance sheets to implement necessary changes to company's financial strategy

- reviewing and negotiating commercial leases
- developing and maintaining relationships with creditors
- planning corporate property and liability coverages
- directing health insurance and workers compensation plans

Jim's Background

Jim is making an impressive start in the financial world as he just been out of college for six years. After graduating with a bachelor's degree in accounting, his first job was as a customer service representative at a major bank, with the task of maintaining consumer satisfaction with the bank's payroll services. He was responsible for sales of business services, processing payrolls, answering all payroll tax questions, and researching payroll histories. Jim left this firm to become the bookkeeper at a midsize manufacturing corporation. After just one year, he became the corporate controller, and then three years later he was a vice president and the finance manager of the firm. Jim left this company because he wanted to be part of a start-up where he could be in on the ground floor and get equity in the firm. This opportunity was not available in his previous job as it was a family-owned company. In the future, Jim would like to become the chief financial officer of the travel firm. In order to get the skills needed for this job, he is currently working on getting his M.B.A. in night school.

Jobs for Money Movers at Medium-Size Businesses

When companies begin to have sufficient business activity, the people working on the money side start to specialize, and financial departments such as accounts payable, accounts receivable, billing, cost accounting, and general accounting begin to emerge. The person in charge of the entire financial function will have the title of controller, treasurer, or vice president of finance, and accountants will be at the head of each department. The major financial workforce is made up of clerks. These are entry-level positions requiring only a high school diploma and a facility for numbers. More and more, however, it is becoming necessary to add computer know-how to the required skills list as companies continue to computerize their financial records. Information is being entered into computers from receipts, bills, and other documents to be stored electronically, as computer printouts, or both. Manual posting to ledgers is rapidly becoming a thing of the past.

Billing and Other Accounting Clerks

Billing clerks keep the records and calculate the charges made for goods or services. In accounting and law firms, these clerks calculate client fees based on the actual time required to perform the task. It is their job to keep track of the accumulated hours and dollar amounts to charge for each job, the type of job performed for a customer, and the percentage of work completed. In hospitals, they have the task of calculating the charges for a patient's stay. At trucking companies, they use rate books to compute shipping charges. Once they have computed the charges, they prepare itemized statements, bills, or invoices depending on the needs of the company.

The jobs of other accounting clerks are also reflected by their titles. Accounts payable clerks are involved in the paying of bills, while accounts receivable clerks handle payments of customers and keep a record of what is owed to the firm. The cost accounting clerks determine the cost of what the firm produces, while the general accounting clerks handle bookkeeping, reports, and all other accounting.

There are more than two million clerks working in accounting positions in the United States. The largest number work for firms providing health, business, and other types of services. This number is not really expected to grow much as computers are increasingly being used to manage account information, and individual clerks are now able to handle more accounts. Just the same, there will be ample opportunity for employment in this area as turnover is relatively high as clerks transfer to other occupations.

Salaries

The salaries of clerks working in accounting vary considerably depending on the firm and area of the country. Median salaries are now approximately $20,000.

Jobs for Financial Mavens at Large Corporations

As the size of a business increases, so does the complexity of the organization of its financial departments. In the largest publicly held firms, there will not only be financial staff at headquarters but also at divisions and subsidiaries. Within America's largest corporations, there are thousands of jobs that will let financial mavens spend their days immersed in money matters. Study the organization chart on the next page for a basic idea of how large single-purpose organizations with no divisions are organized. At the top of the chart is the chief financial officer (CFO), who oversees all the financial departments, helps top managers develop financial and economic policy, and oversees the implementation of these policies.

A CFO with Experience

Tom Calcaterra is a man of many talents. After graduating from college with a bachelor's degree in science and accounting, Tom joined a large public accounting firm as a staff accountant. He

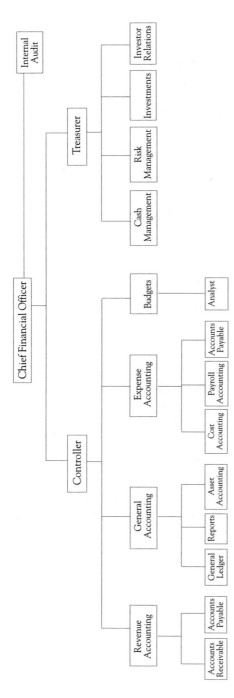

Basic organization chart of a large company with
no divisions or subsidiaries

stayed with this company for twelve years and was promoted to senior manager. If Tom had stayed with the company, his next promotion would have been to partner. Upon leaving his first employer, Tom changed industries and went to work for a foreign-owned company where he became the vice president of finance.

After working for this company for eight years, Tom was ready for another career and industry change. One of the great things about possessing accounting and finance skills is that your knowledge is needed across the spectrum of industries. In 1997 Tom went to work for an employment search firm, joining this company as chief financial officer and secretary. Today there are more than two thousand employees in the company and eight thousand more on contract. In handling his duties, Tom manages a staff of twenty people.

There is no such thing as a typical day in Tom's world, but there are some tasks that he does on a daily basis. Tom spends a great deal of time each day talking on the phone with his field managers, with human resources personnel, and with his subordinates in finance. He generally receives and responds to anywhere between forty and sixty E-mail messages. His company has more than eighty offices across the country, all of which have real estate, legal, computer system, and accounting issues that Tom coordinates and resolves.

On the Job

Tom is the financial "fix-it man" who has his hands on virtually every aspect of the business, because every department in the company needs, uses, and raises money. He has helped open new credit facilities, set up the employees' pension and medical plans, calculated international taxes for overseas customers, and even opened a new location in Mexico.

When Tom first came to this employment search firm, he discovered that its accounting organization was in trouble. Accounts were not being paid on time, and employees were disgruntled over getting late paychecks. Tom went to work and reorganized the internal structure through process reengineering and implemented a management reporting system. He also designed new operating reports for management that linked all aspects of the corporation together.

Virtually everyone in the company knows Tom personally because everything comes back to finance, payroll, and commissions. Tom and his staff are responsible for explaining the commissions processes and calculations to the sales forces. He also does considerable work in investor relations, receiving calls from analysts and shareholders. Whenever the stock is up, analysts call to ask what is going on. Tom is bound by laws that dictate what information he can and can't tell the analysts so that he isn't giving away inside information.

Career Advice

According to Tom, it takes a certain type of person to be successful at finance. You need to be an organized, hard-working individual who enjoys working with and managing people. You also need to possess project management skills. Tom recommends starting your career with a big finance/consulting company and then possibly moving to a smaller boutique firm. He feels it's important to match your personality with the company you work for.

Treasurers and Controllers

The organization chart shows that the treasurer and the controller report directly to the chief financial officer. They are highly trained and experienced senior financial managers. Treasurers are responsible for the receipt, disbursement, and safekeeping of corporate monies. They also review financial reports. Controllers oversee all the accounting departments and direct the preparation of all financial reports.

A Treasurer at a Fortune 500 Company

In order to become a treasurer at a Fortune 500 company, you typically work in a number of other positions learning as much as you can about the financial operation of the company. This is exactly what Mark Edwards did staring as an assistant to the vice president of administration. In this job, he worked with heads of divisions (frozen foods, canned goods, bakery products) of the company in creating and maintaining the assets budget. He also coordinated production planning between the marketing and production departments. Mark was well qualified for these responsibilities, having majored in economics and earned an M.B.A. Plus, he had spent many summers working in canneries, so he had some very practical knowledge of the food industry.

Within a few years, Mark moved entirely to the financial side of the organization and became assistant treasurer reporting to the treasurer. This is typically a training position for future treasurers provided they demonstrate that they have the skills needed to be treasurer. Mark's first responsibility was handling daily cash management. Then over the next few years, he took on new responsibilities every year, adding risk management and then investor relations, in which he was creating the annual report and quarterly reports as well as dealing with buy-side financial analysts. When the treasurer retired, Mark became the new treasurer.

The Job of Treasurer

As treasurer, Mark became responsible for all banking relationships. This involved borrowing and paying off more than $100 million of short-term loans each year and working with more than thirty banks. This was his most important task as treasurer.

Advancing His Career

In business school, Mark set his sights on becoming CFO of a large corporation. He realized this goal a few years after becoming treasurer. As CFO of the company, he had the responsibility of raising capital for stock and bond markets, which involved many trips to New York City, around the country, and even abroad.

A Controller at a Large Manufacturer

Tod Jordan has always been an extremely civic-minded individual. Through these activities, he has contributed to the welfare of the community, brought positive recognition to the companies where he has worked, and has met and worked with community leaders. Tod had a very strong background in accounting when he became controller at this manufacturing company. He graduated from college in accounting, earned his CPA, worked at a very large public accounting firm, and served as controller of a smaller firm. The manufacturing company was so large that there were controllers in every division handling the basic accounting functions. It was Tod's job to see that his department combined and consolidated these statements. His most important job was to set the policy for all division controllers to follow. In addition, Tod was responsible for all corporate level accounting, cash accounting, tax accounting, corporate asset accounting, and budgeting. He set the rules for all budgeting and presented budgets to upper management. Within one year of assuming this position, Tod was elected vice president of the company.

More Financial Managers—
Who They Are and What They Do

Look again at the corporate organization chart, and you will notice how many different departments report to the treasurer and controller. Each of these departments in large corporations has a manager who oversees other departments, with even more managers in charge of them. The number of financial managers in large corporations is enormous, so only a few of these jobs will be described. Pursue your interest in what corporate financial mavens do by talking to people who work in these areas.

Corporate Cash Manager

Jigisha Desai is the cash manager for one of the largest construction companies in the United States. She is very well qualified for this position, with a bachelor's degree in accounting and an M.B.A. in corporate finance. She is also a CCM, or Certified Cash Manager. To achieve this certification you must pass a test that requires intensive study.

Her career in finance began when she accepted a position as an accounting clerk in a Houston newspaper. Jigisha then moved to Los Angeles, where she worked as an accounting supervisor in accounts receivable for a major newspaper. After two and one-half years, she moved to Northern California and took a job with a high-technology company and then her present company.

Jigisha's Responsibilities

As a cash manager, Jigisha is responsible for her company's in and out money flow. She also creates cash flow projections for short-term cash, making sure that there is always enough money to pay the bills. If for some reason the company is short on money, she will make recommendations on how to obtain it. Jigisha is constantly monitoring the cash so that there is never any money just sitting there not earning interest. In addition, she always knows what the market is doing, watching it to make sure the company's investments are secure and to find additional investment opportunities.

Whenever the company decides to do business in a new state, Jigisha is responsible for developing relationships and creating accounts with local banks. She conducts a cost-benefit analysis to determine which options a bank offers will be most valuable to the company. When the company considers acquiring another company, Jigisha must determine how they will pay for the acquisition and whether or not it is a sound investment.

A Typical Day

Jigisha's day starts at seven in the morning; it is earlier than most employees because she follows the New York Stock Exchange. After checking the market, she powers up her computer and logs into the bank's computer, an action that requires a password and gives her real-time market action. She then makes sure that all investments are paid for, determines what will and won't clear that day, and electronically transfers money between the employees' 401(k) funds and their paychecks.

Pluses and Minuses

One of the things that Jigisha enjoys most about her job is getting to work with professional people. Every day brings new excitement and challenges as she works in a dynamic industry where many corporations are merging. The only aspect of Jigisha's job that she doesn't like is the many little problems. She is always receiving phone calls from people who can't cash their checks or who think they were paid incorrectly. It is also difficult to coordinate work and implement changes between the accounts receivable, accounts payable, and paycheck departments. In the future, Jigisha hopes to become the company's treasurer.

Director of Corporate Accounting

Mary Kelly works for a truly giant-sized telecommunications firm with more than sixty thousand employees and $7 billion in revenue. She joined the company eighteen years ago after graduating from college with a degree in mathematical economics and substantial course work with computers, simply because she thought they were fun. Interestingly enough, it was the computer classes that helped her get her initial job with the company.

Mary began working in a computer center where all the disbursement accounting programs were running. Three programs disbursed money: payroll, bills, and employee reimbursements.

Company Benefits

First of all, Mary discovered that she would have the opportunity to take different jobs throughout the company that would enable her to expand her business skills. Over the years, she found that, in many ways, changing positions was like changing companies because the work and work life varied greatly between the departments.

Another appealing benefit was the company's tuition aid program, which paid for any degrees she obtained while employed. She took advantage of this benefit and obtained her M.B.A. by attending night school.

New Jobs

After working in the computer center as a computer operator, Mary became an associate staff manager in a regional accounting office. Her next position was staff manager in the bill and voucher payment office. Mary then made a number of lateral departmental moves, including staff manager of computer operations, staff manager of the regional accounting office, and staff manager of external reporting. Next, she became the district manager of corporate accounting operations and then took the demanding position of statewide markets finance director. Her next move was to the corporate accounting department where, she became the director.

In her position as director of corporate accounting, Mary was responsible for a department of more than 120 people. The department's major task was to close the monthly accounting books and provide financial results to the firm's holding company. The people in her department worked closely with the budget and tax departments and the holding company to ensure that the statements they issued were correct and complete. Mary was deeply involved in the monthly close process. As a result, she would have multiple pre–due date meetings with her team. By the time of the final meeting, her staff had identified all pending and potential issues for the month to review with the chief financial officer. During the close process, Mary worked with both her staff and the CFO whenever a new issue developed or an unknown event occurred. She says that they were constantly challenged to close the books faster, provide better service, and/or do the job for less money.

As director of this department, Mary also worked with the company's external auditors, who were auditing the books for compliance with GAAP (generally accepted accounting practices). She reviewed any issues and concerns that they identified and informed the company and holding company's CFOs of any findings. When conducting an audit, the expectation is that the auditors will find something amiss and some processes or controls which can be strengthened. What is highly undesirable is to have so many findings that the auditors decide to issue a qualified opinion regarding the books, meaning that there were far too many errors and procedural shortcomings. Mary is very pleased to say that the audits prior to her tenure had been clean and they continued to be clean during her time in corporate accounting.

A New Challenge

While Mary was the director of corporate accounting, the CFO asked her to assess the feasibility of replacing the disbursement accounting computer programs with packaged software from a vendor. Some upgrading had been done, but no significant overhaul or upgrading had occurred since she started with the company. After a six-month assessment, Mary recommended the purchase of a software package and then formed a team to implement the new software. As this huge undertaking began, the complexity and scope of the project grew, and it began to take significant time away from her other job areas. In order to successfully handle this project, Mary moved to a new position as the director of financial systems with a team of more than 150 employees.

Career Advice

Mary suggests that you obtain a CPA license as she believes that certification is important to a financial career because it reflects your expertise in finance. Licenses and certification are becoming more important in obtaining jobs with her company.

Financial Manager in a District Office

Pat McCartan is the financial manager in the Mexico district office for a large heavy-equipment manufacturing company. Since Pat is the only employee with a finance background in the office, he handles almost all financial issues in working with the dealers in Mexico. He reviews each dealer's financial condition, meets with dealers to discuss their plans, and assists with strategic planning for the future. Based on these discussions, Pat and the others in the office assess whether or not each dealer is well positioned for the future. When there is a large transaction, he usually handles it through the financial services division of his company, but he may also work with large banks. When special terms are necessary to complete a deal, he works with the dealer to determine what is fair. To handle this job, Pat truly has to be a financial expert. He also has to be a skilled communicator as he speaks with dealers, bankers, coworkers, and customers every day.

Previously, Pat was a financial analyst responsible for the Caribbean–Central America district of his company. He worked with fourteen dealers and was responsible for handling their receivables with his company, assisting the dealers in finding financing for themselves and their customers, and monitoring the financial strength of these dealers.

Starting His Career

Pat started on the road to his present career while he was still in college. First, he worked as a credit analyst trainee at a bank and then as a collection specialist at another bank. Both jobs involved dealing with financial matters similar to the ones in his present job. Pat holds a bachelor's degree in finance and has taken continuing education classes through his company to build his negotiating skills for future jobs.

The Future

In the immediate future, Pat would like to become a finance representative working in the field. This position would involve traveling to dealers and working with them on a more personal basis. In the long run, he hopes to get into management in the organization.

Career Advice

Pat's advice to anyone thinking about a career in finance is to try to find internships that will give you solid work experience for your resume.

What It's Like on the Job

As a money mover on the financial side in business, your working conditions will vary from firm to firm and from office to office depending on the type of company in which you are employed. If you are the financial manager at a small furniture store, you may share an office or even a cubicle with one or more people. If you are an entry-level financial manager at a larger corporation, you will, at a minimum, have your own cubicle. As you progress in your career, your work space will become larger, and you are likely to have your own office close to top managers and to departments that develop the financial data these managers need.

Financial managers typically work forty-hour weeks, but many work longer hours. In addition, attendance at meetings of financial and economic associations and similar activities is often required. In very large corporations, some traveling to subsidiary firms, banks, and customers may be necessary.

A Look at the Qualifications Financial Careers Require

If you want to become a financial manager, you will usually need to have a bachelor's degree in accounting, finance, or business administration with an emphasis on accounting or finance. Many companies prefer job candidates who have a master of business administration (M.B.A.) degree. While it is possible to find a job on the financial side with a high school diploma, you are limited initially to clerking jobs. Once you get experience, it is possible to get promoted. Nevertheless, promotions come much easier to individuals who have continued their education.

Due to the increasing complexity of worldwide trade, the constantly changing federal and state laws and regulations, and the onslaught of new, complex financial instruments, it has become vital for financial managers to continue their education. Firms often provide opportunities for workers to increase their knowledge and skills through continuing education courses, seminars and conferences, and even graduate school programs. Because of the technological revolution, knowledge of computer applications, especially spreadsheets, is essential.

Certificate and License Programs

Financial managers who wish to broaden their skills and exhibit their competency in specialized fields can do so by obtaining a certificate. For example, the Association for Investment Management and Research confers the Chartered Financial Analyst (CFA) designation to investment professionals who have a bachelor's degree, pass three test levels, and have three or more years of experience in the field. The National Association of Credit Management administers a three-part certification program for business credit professionals that leads to becoming a Certified Credit Executive (CCE). Another important designation is CPA, which was discussed in Chapter 2.

A Look at Salaries for Financial Managers

Salary levels depend upon the manager's experience and the size and location of the organization; they are likely to be higher in larger organizations and cities. Many financial managers in upper management positions receive additional compensation in the form of bonuses, which vary with the size of the firm. Here is a look at the recent annual earnings for several financial manager positions. These figures include bonuses.

Chief financial officer	$142,900
Vice president of finance	$138,000
Treasurer	$122,500
Assistant treasurer	$88,400
Controller	$85,100
Assistant controller	$56,200
Senior analyst	$55,600

Cash manager	$51,600
Analyst	$40,500
Assistant cash manager	$38,500

A Look at What the Future Holds

Similar to other managerial occupations, the number of applicants for financial management positions is expected to exceed the number of job openings, resulting in competition for jobs. Financial mavens with a graduate degree, a strong analytical background, and knowledge of various aspect of financial management, such as asset management and information and technology management, should enjoy the best opportunities for jobs in financial management. Developing expertise in a rapidly growing industry, such as health care, could also be an advantage in the job market.

Through the year 2005, employment opportunities for financial managers is expected to increase faster than the average for all other occupations. The twentieth century has experienced corporate restructuring and consolidation that has helped firms to reduce their number of middle managers in an effort to become more efficient and competitive; luckily this downsizing trend is nearing completion.

In the long run, some areas are expected to show continued growth. Management consultant positions are expected to flourish for accountants, budget analysts, and other financial types who possess business experience with marketing and technology. One additional and exciting new area of growth for financial types is in the international marketplace. As trade increases across the globe, there will be more job opportunities in areas such as China, East Asia, and the former Soviet Union republics.

More Career Information

For information about financial management careers, contact:

Financial Management Association, International
College of Business Administration
University of South Florida
Tampa, FL 33620-5500

For information about financial careers in business credit management and institutions offering certificates and graduate courses in credit and financial management, contact:

National Association of Credit Management
8815 Centre Park Dr.
Columbia, MD 21045

For information about the Chartered Financial Analyst program, contact:

Association for Investment Management and Research
5 Boar's Head Ln.
P.O. Box 3668
Charlottesville, VA 22903

For information about careers in treasury management, from entry level to chief financial officer, and the Certified Cash Manager and Certified Treasury Executive programs, contact:

Treasury Management Association
7315 Wisconsin Ave., Suite 600
West Bethesda, MD 20814

CHAPTER TEN

Handling Money for the Government

Where the Jobs Are

J ust as businesses and banks have jobs that let people spend their workday dealing with money, so do federal, state, and local governments, which all together employ one in every six Americans. While you can find jobs that are similar to those in the private sector, such as accountants, auditors, controllers, bookkeepers, economists, budget analysts, and clerks, many government jobs that would appeal to money movers are quite unique. You could be an engraver, bank examiner, secret service agent, tax assessor, and tax collector, to name just a few of these jobs. In this chapter, we will describe the government departments that deal with money and some of the jobs in these departments. Although accountants and auditors can be found at every government agency at every level, we will not focus on these jobs, as they were discussed in Chapter 2.

The Federal Government as Your Employer

The federal government is the largest employer in the United States; it has well over three million civilian employees, not counting the millions of administrators, teachers, and police that are paid by state, county, or city governments. With such vast numbers of employees, numerous jobs open every day all across the country. It has been estimated that the federal government hires more than three hundred thousand people each year. While you might think that the majority of federal jobs are located in Washington, D.C., in reality, only 14 percent of the positions are located there; the other 86 percent are spread throughout the country.

The variety of positions that you could hold while working for the federal government is virtually endless. It is possible to have a position in which you manage, budget, or distribute money in literally every government department. Let's look at four departments where you would work specifically with money.

Jobs with the Federal Reserve System

If you were to work for the Federal Reserve System, you would be working for the central bank of the United States. You could have a say in the nation's financial policies, for one of the duties of the Reserve is to conduct these policies. Or you could be involved in the supervision and regulation of banking institutions to make sure they are safe and stable and protect consumers' credit rights. The Reserve also maintains the stability of the financial system and plays a very important role in operating the nation's payments system.

Jobs with the Federal Trade Commission

The purpose of the Federal Trade Commission (FTC) is to ensure that our nation's markets function competitively and are vigorous, efficient, and free of unnecessary restrictions. The commission enforces a variety of antitrust and consumer protection laws. While the FTC primarily hires attorneys and economists to accomplish its consumer protection, antitrust, and competition missions, it also has a limited number of positions for other types of professional, administrative, and support positions. In a support position, you could be a clerk or typist and earn an average salary of $19,531.

Jobs with the Department of the Treasury

The Department of the Treasury has two major components: the departmental offices, which are responsible for creating government policy and managing the department and the operating bureaus that carry out the specific tasks assigned to the department. The basic functions of the Department of the Treasury include managing federal finances; collecting taxes, duties, and monies paid to and due to the United States; and paying all bills of the United States. This department is so large that we will look at several of its divisions.

The Bureau of Alcohol, Tobacco, and Firearms (ATF)

This bureau was established on July 1, 1972, under the Internal Revenue Service. It has law enforcement and compliance divisions for alcohol, explosives, and firearms. On the money side, it collects alcohol and tobacco excise taxes and ensures the collection of federal taxes on distilled spirits, beer, wine, and tobacco products and assists state and local law enforcement agencies upon request. The principal occupations with the ATF are alcohol, tobacco, and firearms inspector and treasury enforcement agent (special agent).

Office of the Comptroller of the Currency (OCC)

The OCC was established in 1863 as a way to regulate the National Banking System. As the administrator of nationally chartered banks, it is responsible for the execution of laws, rules, and regulations that govern the operations of national banks. As the OCC employs more than twenty-three hundred bank examiners nationwide, it clearly offers financial mavens many career opportunities.

The OCC is also responsible for approving and denying applications for new bank charters and branches as well as capital or other changes in the corporate or banking structure. It will take supervisory action against banks that do not obey the laws and against those with unsound banking practices. If you were employed by the OCC, you would probably have one of the following titles: bank examiner, financial economist, accountant, or computer specialist. As an economist, you could expect an average annual income of close to $60,000.

Internal Revenue Service (IRS)

Everyone is familiar with the IRS, which is the government agency responsible for determining, assessing, and collecting money from personal and corporate income taxes; excise, estate, and gift taxes; and employment taxes for the nation's Social Security system. The IRS was originally formed to pay for the Civil War. Although it was declared unconstitutional to tax for about twenty years, the IRS was reinstated in 1913. Today, it is the largest of the Treasury bureaus. While working for the IRS, you might have one of the following titles: tax specialist, revenue officer, revenue agent, tax auditor, taxpayer service specialist, Treasury enforcement agent (special agent), or attorney. There are more than 15,730 individuals currently employed by the IRS; their average annual salary is $48,304.

United States Mint

Within the Mint there are jobs that should really appeal to money movers, as it has the responsibility for creating all of the nation's coinage. The Mint has facilities in Philadelphia, Denver, San Francisco, and West Point, along with many other locations. Mint employees also maintain United States gold bullion reserves at the West Point Bullion Depository and the Fort Knox Bullion Depository.

In addition to manufacturing and maintaining our money, the Mint manages extensive commercial marketing programs. Its product line includes special coin sets for collectors, national medals, American eagle gold and silver bullion coins, and commemorative coins marking national events such as the bicentennial of the Constitution. If you worked in this area of the Mint, you would most likely be called a marketing specialist and be responsible for designing, producing, and marketing special coinage—literally devising ways to sell money to make more money.

Bureau of Engraving and Printing (BEP)

This department is also closely involved with money, as it is responsible for printing our paper money, sometimes referred to as the *greenback*. Other responsibilities include designing and manufacturing many postage stamps, customs stamps, and revenue stamps; designing, engraving and printing Treasury bills, notes and bonds, and other government securities; and designing, engraving and printing commissions, permits, and certificates of awards. While working for the BEP, you might have such job titles as computer specialist, engineer, chemist, plate printer, electrician, security specialist, contract specialist, machinist, or engraver. If you are an employee of this department, it is possible to be an accountant or even an engineer and still work with or create greenbacks.

Financial Management Service (FMS)

This service is responsible for one of the oldest and most basic functions of the Department of the Treasury: it receives and disburses all public money, maintains government accounts, and prepares daily and monthly reports on the status of government finances. The FMS also improves multiple cash management systems throughout the government. Additionally, the FMS receives all money collected through taxes and duties, manages the government's central accounting and financial system, provides central payment services for most government programs, and settles claims for both lost and/or forged government checks.

The FMS invests Social Security and other trust funds. It provides banking services that manage the government's cash resources. Believe it or not, the FMS even destroys unfit currency and helps to settle claims for burned and mutilated currency. You could work for the FMS as an accountant, management analyst, program analyst, or financial management specialist, to name just a few jobs.

Bureau of the Public Debt (BPD)

Money movers may wish to investigate this bureau, which borrows the money needed to operate the federal government. The BPD issues and services United States Treasury bonds, savings, and special securities. It also services registered accounts and makes calculations to pay the appropriate interest when it's due. Another branch of the Treasury working with bonds and securities is the United States Savings Bonds Division, which promotes the sale and retention of United States savings bonds. If you worked for either of these departments, you could have the job title of accountant or computer specialist.

United States Secret Service

Believe it or not, you could even have a career in finance while working for the Secret Service. This service was originally created to stop the counterfeiting of paper currency during the Civil War. Although the Secret Service is best known for its role in protecting the president, it also enforces the laws that protect our currency. It guards the integrity of our currency and investigates crimes that involve United States securities, coinage, credit and debt card fraud, and electronic funds transfer fraud. While working for the Secret Service, you might be called a treasury enforcement agent (special agent) or a uniformed division officer.

Office of Thrift Supervision (OTS)

This office is in charge of regulating all federal- and state-chartered savings institutions that belong to the Savings Association Insurance Fund (SAIF). While the OTS is headquartered in Washington, D.C., it maintains a staff that works out of local offices in five different regions.

A Look at How the Federal Government Pays Employees

When financial mavens think about working for—and getting paid by—the federal government, they need to understand that they will probably be paid under the General Schedule (GS), which is composed of fifteen grades numbered GS-1 through GS-15. Each grade has a salary range of ten steps that is defined by the level of responsibility, type of work, and the various qualifications required for each position. Employees are typically promoted through steps 1, 2, and 3 at the rate of one step per year. In steps 4, 5, and 6, they move up one step every two years. And in 7, 8, and 9, they move up one step every three years.

In addition to the General Schedule, the federal government has what is called the Executive Schedule (ES) for its senior-level employees working in the executive branch. The salaries in this schedule are higher because the government is hoping to attract first-rate managers who have an exceptional education and prior work experience. The third and final schedule that makes up the pay scale for the federal government is called the Senior Executive Schedule (SES), which is for the very top levels of government and is limited to only eighty-five hundred employees. Members of this schedule are not paid as much as those in the Executive Schedule, but they are eligible for additional compensation and benefits based upon their performance. These performance awards can amount to as much as 20 percent of an employee's base salary.

General Schedule Employees and Mean Salaries

Grade	# Employees	Mean Salary
GS-1	370	$13,038
GS-2	2,443	$14,880
GS-3	25,764	$17,003
GS-4	97,627	$19,597
GS-5	166,176	$22,133
GS-6	108,556	$24,804
GS-7	140,609	$27,274
GS-8	41,034	$30,892
GS-9	145,110	$32,973
GS-10	16,090	$37,700
GS-11	210,657	$39,925
GS-12	239,332	$48,051
GS-13	159,427	$58,230
GS-14	85,490	$69,539
GS-15	40,325	$83,925
Total	1,479,010	Average $39,070

Employment Outlook for Federal Government Jobs

It is important to note that while government salaries are generally more for low-level positions and less for upper levels of management than their equivalent positions in the private sector, exceptional benefits and job security provide strong incentives to work for the government. You must also remember that while there appear to be many positions opening each year, the federal government employment levels rise very slowly. It is projected that total federal employment will increase by only two hundred thousand people over the next ten years—a small number when compared to the number of individuals currently employed. Overall, the employment outlook for positions federal jobs is fair.

How to Find a Job with the Federal Government

Because the United States government employs just over three million civilians, it is not surprising that there are thousands of jobs available all the time, all across the country and even in foreign countries. While there are many jobs available, they are often difficult to find because there is no one central government listing of all open positions. The following is a list of books that you will find useful in obtaining your dream job.

Find a Federal Job Fast! by Ronald L. Krannich and Caryl Rae Krannich. Impact Publications, Woodbridge, Virginia.

Guide to Federal Jobs, Second Edition. Editor-In-Chief: Rod W. Durgin. Resource Directories, Toledo, Ohio.

How To Get a Federal Job by David E. Waelde. Fedhelp Publications, P. O. Box 15204, Dept. GOF, Washington, DC 20003.

A Special Job Program

In 1990 the federal government began a new program to attract college graduates into civil service jobs. The Administrative

Careers with America (ACWA) program supports more than one hundred different entry-level jobs with annual salaries ranging from $16,000 to $30,000. Positions are found in six categories: benefits review, tax, legal, business, finance, and management.

To qualify for this program, you must either have a bachelor's degree (or anticipate having one in eight months) or possess a minimum of three full years of prior work experience. There is also a written test for each of the occupational groups that you must pass in order to gain employment.

More Job Information

You should visit the federal government's Employment Information Highway, which is available at the Office of Personnel Management (OPM); there are more than forty-four offices nationwide. These offices keep a list of job openings at the federal level and will help guide applicants through the job search process. You can phone or write the OPM to request a copy of the job listings. If you have access to the Internet, you will find OPM at http://www.fjob.mail.opm.gov. On this site you can read about current openings and request job applications.

Many government agencies have direct-hire authority and will fill positions rapidly without ever listing their openings with the OPM. In order to find those positions, you will need to keep in contact with the agencies in which you are interested. It is often a good idea to write or call the department heads or supervisors and speak with them directly.

Another way to discover employment opportunities is to buy, subscribe to, or find a local library copy of such publications as the *Federal Jobs Digest* or *Federal Career Opportunities*. The *Digest* is a biweekly newspaper that tracks federal job vacancies and contains articles about job fairs, including those on college campuses. The *Opportunities* publication focuses on jobs at the GS-5 level and above.

Financial Jobs with State and Local Governments

State and local governments are organized very similarly to the federal government. The state has a governor (the equivalent of the president) and multiple departments designed to manage different aspects of state business, including money.

Department of Finance

All states have a Department of Finance. It may be found in different segments of the government or called a different name, but it is always there and a good place for money movers to look for jobs. Most financial departments are responsible for enforcing the state's laws relating to state-licensed banks, state-licensed savings and loan associations, trust companies, state-licensed offices of foreign banks, issuers of travelers checks and payment instruments (money orders), transmitters of money abroad, state-licensed credit unions, and state-licensed industrial loan companies.

Bureau of State Audits

This bureau serves to ensure the effective and efficient administration and management of public funds and programs. It provides independent, nonpartisan, accurate, and timely assessments of the state government's financial and operational activities.

Department of Economic and Community Development

This state agency is responsible for promoting economic growth and community development. While working there, you could help to create long-term economic plans and develop strategies and programs to attract and retain businesses and jobs. Or you could choose a job ensuring that your state's tax dollars are used efficiently by measuring performance, calculating quantitative measurements, or tracking results.

A Brief Look at State and Local Government Salaries

How much you earn working for a state government depends greatly on the state. The same is true for positions with both counties and cities. Generally the larger the government unit, the larger the salary. Financial mavens will earn more in New York and California than in Alabama and Arkansas. In the same way, jobs dealing with money will pay far better in San Francisco than in the much smaller town of Rhinelander, Wisconsin.

Finding a State or Local Job

When searching for a job on the financial side in state, county, or city governments, be sure to check departments that have names similar to the following: Budget Department, Department of Administration, Division of Administrative Services, Division of Finance, Division of General Services, and Office of the Commissioner. Most state government jobs are found in the state capital or large metropolitan areas. Expressing a willingness to relocate to other areas may improve your chances for obtaining a job. The larger the county or city, the more jobs there will be for money movers.

Finding employment with the government at the state, county, and even city levels can be challenging, but it is generally easier than at the federal level. For employment listings, you can contact your state's equivalent of the Department of Employment Relations Information, an organization that lists current employment opportunities. You can also conduct an on-line search of your state government's Web site. Finally, in state and county capitols and city government offices, you will be able to pick up employment listings and view job openings on bulletin boards.

An Overview of Government Job Opportunities

It is important for financial mavens and other money movers to remember that the federal government and your local and state government offer a vast number of careers with considerable job security. They also offer opportunities to steadily climb a career ladder to more responsible and higher-paying positions. As we move into the twenty-first century, the number of government jobs working with money is growing at a slow but steady pace. While working for your city, county, state, or even the federal government may not always pay as much as the private sector, you will typically enjoy a higher level of job security and benefits. And do remember, when you take a government job, you are contributing to the smooth running of our country.

CHAPTER ELEVEN

Finding Even More Jobs Dealing with Money

S ome people want to work with words; others are attracted to careers where they can work with nature, children, or their hands. True happiness for money movers is having a job in which they directly or indirectly manage, deal with, or handle money all day long. In this book, we have described many careers that are good choices for you. Here are a few more career ideas for financial mavens.

Cashiers Handle Money

Remember how much fun you had handling money as a child when you played games like Monopoly and Pay Day. As a cashier, you could spend your workdays handling money in a supermarket, department store, gasoline service station, movie theater, restaurant, or any other place where people purchase or pay for goods or services. Cashiers used to ring up sales using a cash register, manually entering the price of each item the consumer was buying. This task is now being handled by scanners and computers in most establishments; however, cashiers are still handling money as they make change. They also are dealing with money in the form of credit cards, debit cards, and checks. Although specific job duties vary by employer, cashiers are usually assigned to a register and given a drawer containing a bank of money at the beginning of their shifts. They must count their "bank" to ensure that it contains the correct amount and that there is an adequate supply of change. At the end of their shift, they once again count the drawer's contents and compare the totals with sales data. Depending on the place they work, cashiers often have other duties. For example, in supermarkets they weigh produce and other bulk foods, in convenience stores they handle money orders, and in many stores they handle returns and exchanges.

Jobs as cashiers are typically entry-level positions requiring little or no previous work experience and no specific educational background. They offer an opportunity to work with money and can serve as a stepping-stone to advancement to head cashier, cash office clerk, or other positions in a company. There is almost always an opportunity to get a job as a cashier, as the occupation is huge and has a high turnover.

Training

Nearly all cashiers are trained on the job. In small firms, the training is typically handled by an experienced worker. The first day is usually spent observing the operation and becoming familiar with all procedures and policies. After this, the trainee is assigned to a register under the supervision of a more experienced employee. In larger firms, cashiers may spend several days in classes before being assigned to a register.

Earnings

Cashiers' earnings vary from minimum wage to several times that amount, especially in areas where there is intense competition for workers.

A Cashier at a Video Store

Ann Gisler works as a cashier in a large video store. She advises future cashiers to take a computer class because most cash registers are now computerized. In stores with scanners, the cashier passes the product's code over the scanning device, which transmits the code number to a computer. The computer identifies the item and its price. In other establishments, like the one where Ann is employed, cashiers manually enter the code into a computer, and a description of the item and its price appear on the screen. Ann also cautions prospective cashiers to brush up on their math as it isn't wise to rely totally on the computer. Besides working as a cashier, Ann logs returned videos into the computer and does some shelving.

A Lawyer Who Is an Estate Planner

Lawyers can have a career that focuses on both the law and working with money. In this category are tax lawyers and those who specialize in estate planning. James W. Smyth is an attorney who helps his clients plan their estates. His job is to analyze the tax consequences and personal consequences involved in leaving money and other possessions to those who will inherit an estate. Because the laws are complex in this area, he must explain them carefully to his clients. James firmly believes that each client knows his or her family best and the issues that are important in resolving how the estate will be left. He tells the clients the pros and cons of different estate plans and lets them decide which plan is most suitable for them.

James works a sixty- to eighty-hour week. Much of his time is involved with keeping on top of the laws and all the complex technical areas associated with estate planning. He points out that a good estate planner needs more than a law degree because that only takes care of the legal side. On the financial side, he frequently works hand in hand with an accountant. In this profession, James says that it is extremely important to be ethical and not receive any financial reward tied to the clients' estate planning decisions.

James likes his profession because it gives him an opportunity to help families. He is grateful that technology has made it possible for middle-class families to have customized estate plans—not just the wealthy. He dislikes the fact that it is difficult to balance his long hours and family life. In order to succeed as an estate planner, James believes that lawyers need to be very creative and have a technical mind set.

Tax Consultants Need to Be Financial Mavens

Independent tax consultant Diane Ingram gives advice to people so they can file the best possible return based on their income. When it is time to file taxes, she prepares a variety of tax forms for clients using the information they have provided. What Diane likes most about her career is that working as an independent tax consultant gives her the time and freedom to work at her own pace. She is almost always able to work without feeling pressed for time. It also gives her the opportunity to give each individual client sufficient attention to produce the best possible return. However, what Diane dislikes most about her job is clients who are not prepared to provide her with the information essential to making a fair and accurate determination of what tax approach would benefit them. Sometimes, she has to meet with clients five or six times before they are able to provide her with the necessary information to start on their taxes. Then it becomes a problem to complete them within a reasonable period of time.

Some of the responsibilities of Diane's job include being a good record keeper and keeping up-to-date on the tax code. Fortunately, technology has made these tasks easier, as she can use the computer to create returns and to receive updated material on the tax code from government units and other sources.

Earnings

Diane's earning potential is unlimited. Because she works for herself, she sets her own prices and chooses the number of clients with whom she will work.

Career Advice

According to Diane, future tax consultants need to become avid readers to keep up with all the new information that is constantly being put out on taxes. It's the only way they'll truly be able to prepare good returns for their clients.

Auctioneers Sell to the Highest Bidder

If you can speak clearly in front of large audiences and have a high level of self-confidence, then you might want to be an auctioneer. An auction is a sales event during which people make bids for specific items; for example, at a fine arts auction, people might bid for antiques, jewelry, and other collectibles. The auctioneer is the individual responsible for calling out the starting and ensuing prices of the item being sold.

To prepare for an auction, an auctioneer must be aware of what is being sold. He or she must study the auction's catalog and learn which items are the most important. Preparation also includes talking with department people about the items to be auctioned.

Auctioneering is not a skill or trade you learn in school, rather it is one learned by watching other auctioneers and then developing your own style. A very important characteristic for auctioneers is to have confidence in themselves. One way to gain confidence is to have a great deal of knowledge regarding the items you are auctioning; for example, if you were auctioning fine arts, it would help to have a degree in fine arts, to have worked in an art museum, or to have been a collector yourself.

Ticket Sellers Are Money Handlers

If you worked as a ticket seller, you would be responsible for selling tickets to customers for events, shows, movies, lotteries, and even more. You would typically operate ticket-dispensing machines and answer customers' questions. You might work for a large ticket selling company like Ticketmaster, where you book tickets on a computer while speaking with customers on the phone. You might also work at the counter of a movie theater or sporting arena, where you would have face-to-face contact with your customers while you sell them the tickets they desire. Like cashiers, nearly one-half of all ticket sellers earn minimum wage and work part-time. Virtually all this work is done indoors at desks with phones or in booths or behind counters.

Desk Clerks Prepare Bills

Your desire to work with money could lead you to become a clerk at a hotel or motel. These desk clerks perform a wide variety of services for their guests. As a desk clerk, you will register arriving guests and assign them rooms and check guests out at the end of their stay. It will frequently be necessary for you to prepare and explain the bill of charges as well as process payments. You will always be in the public eye, and through your attitude and behavior, you will greatly influence the public's impression of the establishment. If guests report problems with their rooms, you must contact members of the housekeeping or maintenance staff to correct them.

In some smaller hotels and motels, you may even perform the work of a bookkeeper, advance reservation agent, cashier, laundry attendant, and telephone switchboard operator. While there are schools dedicated to training people for the hotel industry, they are primarily for management. As a clerk you will earn minimum wage or higher and will need to possess a high school diploma.

Detectives Can Investigate Financial Dealings

Have you ever considered being a private detective or investigator? If you became a detective, you could perform a vast variety of services. You could assist attorneys, businesses, and the public with a variety of problems, including protecting businesses and their employees, customers, and guests from theft, vandalism, and disorder, as well as gathering evidence for trials, tracing debtors, or conducting background investigations. You could specialize in the finance field, where you might use your accounting skills to investigate the financial standing of a company or locate funds stolen by an embezzler. Or you could search for assets after fraud or theft in order to recover damages awarded by a court. To become a financial investigator it would be helpful to have a background in accounting and even law enforcement. Your income will depend upon your level of expertise. It can be substantial if you share in the moneys you have recovered.

Property Managers Are Financial Managers

Today many businesses and investors own real estate that produces income and profits if it is managed correctly. For this reason, property managers perform an important function in increasing and maintaining the value of real estate investments for investors. If you were to become a property manager, you would oversee the performance of income-producing commercial and residential properties. You might even manage the communal property and services of condominium and community associations. You would handle the financial operations of the property, which involves seeing that mortgages, taxes, insurance premiums, payroll, and maintenance bills are paid on time. In addition, you would supervise the preparation of financial statements and periodically report to the owners on the status of the property, occupancy rates, dates of lease expirations, and other matters. To become a property manager for a business it is almost essential that you have either a degree in finance or at least substantial course work in accounting. While it is possible to become a manager with only a high school diploma, it is becoming increasingly rare.

Financial Writers Know About Money

In newspapers, books, and magazines there are always articles discussing financial issues and how individuals should handle their money. If you were a financial writer, you would conduct extensive research for your books and articles. You might write a weekly column for your paper or even a book that discusses the latest stock market action or suggests useful and lucrative ways for individuals to invest their money. Many financial writers are also needed to prepare technical material for mutual funds, brokerage houses, and banks. And each and every one of these articles deals with money in some way. To become a financial writer you will need to have a degree in journalism or a related field such as creative writing or literature. It would be best to have a degree in finance as well; however, substantial course work in this area should suffice.

Still More Careers

The more you notice where money is being handled and financial activities are taking place, the longer your list of careers for financial mavens like yourself will be. The following list provides a few more careers to investigate.

- tollgate collectors
- teachers of business and accounting classes
- clerks in stores
- claims adjusters
- credit bureau workers
- purchasing agents
- compensation managers
- economists
- estimators
- financial aid directors at colleges
- insurance agents
- check cashing firm employees
- rental clerks
- welfare eligibility workers
- television and radio financial commentators

Overview of Job Opportunities

The future will always be bright for financial mavens seeking jobs that allow them to be paid for working in some way with money. Even when the economy is not robust, there will be jobs because so much money handling is essential in today's world. Accountants will always be required to keep financial records, and individuals will be involved in the buying and selling of securities and the management of small and large financial portfolios. Banks will require employees in myriad capacities to handle money and so will businesses, the government, and just about every organization. Some jobs, especially those in investment banking firms, venture capital firms, and upper management levels of major corporations and banks will always be extremely competitive. However, as long as "money makes the world go round," financial mavens and other money movers can look forward to having a great number of satisfying career choices.

About the Authors

Marjorie Eberts and Margaret Gisler have been writing together professionally for eighteen years. They are prolific freelance authors with more than sixty books in print. Besides writing career books, the two authors have written textbooks, beginning readers, and study skills books for schoolchildren. They also write a syndicated education column, "Dear Teacher," which appears in newspapers throughout the country. This is the second career book that Mary McGowan has written and the fourth for Maria Olson.

Writing this book was a special pleasure for all the authors because it gave them the opportunity to talk to so many financial mavens who are handling money in this country. It was refreshing to see how much all of these people contribute on a daily basis to the success of our economy.

Marjorie Eberts and Mary McGowan hold bachelor's and master's degrees from Stanford University. Margaret Gisler received her bachelor's degree from Ball State and her graduate degrees from Butler University. Maria Olson received her bachelor's degree in business from Indiana University.